Introduction

"In these days of endless national wealth and materialism, of rising crime, bribery, divorce, drunkenness, dishonesty, murder, adultery, and general disregard for God—THESE ARE THE DAYS FOR READING THE ANCIENT PROPHETS. For they lived in the same atmosphere of personal, national, and international arrogance against the God of heaven—of disregard and wilful ignorance of Him— as we do today." So writes Ken Taylor in the preface of *Living Prophecies*. Anyone who wants to make an honest appraisal of the world's spiritual state today, with a view to the outcome, would do well to study the prophetic books of the Old Testament. Christians especially can learn much from the prophets, because their messages, whether foretelling or forthtelling, were directed primary to God's people.

You may not be familiar with the books of the minor prophets, because they are not well known as such. Let this be both a challenge and inspiration to you. As you begin your study of the minor prophets of Judah, why not determine that you are going to let God speak to you through *this* portion of His holy Word? Remember, not *some* but *every* Scripture

> was given to us by inspiration from God and is useful to teach us what is true and to make us realize what is wrong in our lives; it straightens us out and helps us do what is right. It is God's way of making us well prepared at every point, fully equipped to do good to everyone (2 Ti 3:16-17, TLB).

Suggestions for Study

1. Get in the good habit of using pencil and paper freely in all your study. Record your observations as you read the Bible passage of the lesson. Do not hesitate to make small notations (e.g., underlining a key word or phrase) in your Bible. A pencil is one of your best eyes! Write out the answers to questions in the manual.

2. Read all the Bible references cited in the manual. There is no substitute for letting the Bible speak for itself.

Note: The basic version referred to throughout this manual is the King James Version. It is very important for your analytical studies that you consistently use the same translation from lesson to lesson. The question may be asked, "Should I refer to a modern paraphrase, and if

1

so, when?" A sound procedure is this:

ANALYZE a basic translation (e.g., King James[1])

COMPARE a modern paraphrase (e.g., *The Living Bible*)

3. Do not rush through the preparatory Lesson 1. Your analysis of the actual Bible text, beginning with Lesson 2, will be more fruitful if you first learn well the "language" of these Bible books.

4. Study carefully the charts and diagrams in the lessons. This writer has included in all the books of this self-study series many such visual aids because he is convinced that such eye-gate devices are effective helps for clarification, impression, methodicalness, and context orientation. *Survey charts* (e.g., Chart E) give an overview of the Bible book or section, so that you will be aware of the surrounding context in the Bible. *Historical charts* (e.g., Chart A) furnish setting of the Bible book. *Analytical charts* (e.g., Chart M) provide a work sheet on which to record one's observations and outlines of a particular passage.[2]

5. Be willing to spend time—that precious commodity!—in all your studies. A. W. Tozer once said, "God has not bowed to our nervous haste nor embraced the methods of our machine age. The man who will know God must give time to Him." Diligent Bible study is work, but it is wonderfully rewarding. Read Hebrews 5:11—6:2, which warns that a Christian will not grow spiritually if he does not advance from the "milk" to "strong meat" stage of instruction.

6. Be hungry for the spiritual food of God's Word. It has been well said, "If you want food for your soul, you must have soul for the food."

7. Let a dependence on the Holy Spirit underlie all your Bible study. He who inspired the writers of the Scriptures wants to enlighten you as a student of those Scriptures, to bring forth eternal fruit in your life. (Read Jn 16:12-15 and 1 Cor 2:12-13.)

Suggestions to Group Leaders

1. Your Bible study group should have a *leader*, whose task it is to make the sessions interesting, clear, and prac-

---

1. A highly recommended new translation is the New American Standard Bible (NASB).
2. The analytical chart method is fully described in Irving L. Jensen, *Independent Bible Study*.

tical. The leader should determine how much of each lesson in the manual should be studied each time (some lessons, because of the material covered, may be broken down into smaller units). He should lead the discussions (or assign discussion leaders) and encourage the doing of homework assignments which he might give.

2. At the beginning of the group session *review* the previous lesson.

3. Everyone should be encouraged to *participate* in discussion, including the asking of *any kind* of question related to the lesson.

4. Keep looking for everyday *applications* of the Bible text. Someone has written, "To look is one thing. To see what you look at is another. To understand what you see is a third. To learn from what you understand is still something else. But to act on what you learn is what really matters."

5. In group study it is very helpful to have large reproductions of the *charts* (e.g., on chalkboard) in full view of everyone for the frequent references to context or setting which arise when studying books like these. The use of overhead projectors for displaying charts in group study is highly recommended.

6. At the end of the hour *summarize* the highlights of the lesson.

Publisher's Note

Enlarged charts related to the lessons of this study guide are available in *Jensen's Bible Study Charts* (Chicago: Moody, 1981). They were originally published in three volumes (Vol. 1, General Survey; Vol. 2, Old Testament; Vol. 3, New Testament).

The 8½ x 11" charts are especially valuable for Bible study groups, and can be reproduced as Xerox copies or as transparencies for overhead projectors. Selected transparencies are included.

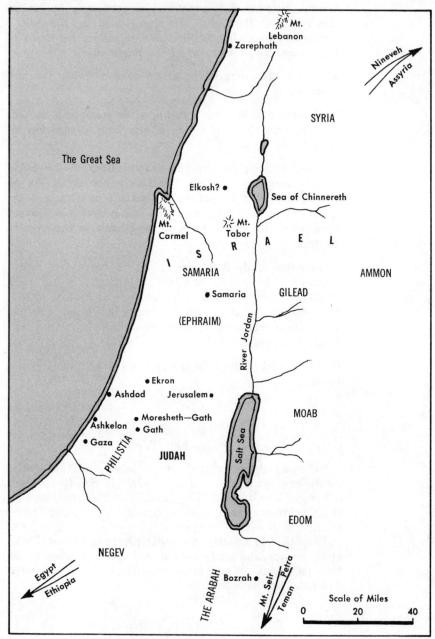

Mt. Lebanon

Zarephath

Nineveh

Assyria

SYRIA

The Great Sea

Elkosh?

Sea of Chinnereth

Mt. Carmel

Mt. Tabor

I S R A E L

SAMARIA

AMMON

Samaria

GILEAD

(EPHRAIM)

River Jordan

Ekron

Ashdod

Jerusalem

Moresheth—Gath

Ashkelon

Gath

Gaza

PHILISTIA

JUDAH

MOAB

Salt Sea

EDOM

NEGEV

Egypt

Ethiopia

Bozrah

Mt. Seir

Petra

Teman

THE ARABAH

Scale of Miles

0   20   40

Background of the Minor Prophets of Judah

SIX OF THE TWELVE MINOR PROPHETS

MINISTERED TO THE SOUTHERN KINGDOM

PRIOR TO THE BABYLONIAN CAPTIVITY.

Before we study each of their books, it will help to learn something of the setting in which Old Testament prophets served God as His spokesmen to His people.

The prophets did not preach in a vacuum. Each spoke to definite needs of the people, as these were disclosed by God through revelation. It should not surprise us as we study their books that the spiritual needs of the people living almost three millennia ago were the same types of needs as today. For human nature is that changeless. In a very real sense Obadiah and Joel and all the other prophets are speaking now *to us*.

I. THE PROPHETIC MINISTRY

The offices of judge, prophet, priest, and king were all important positions in the commonwealth of Israel.[1] Let us inquire into some of the distinctive functions of one of these—the prophet.

The word "prophet" is an important word in the Bible, for it is one of the few official titles given to men of God who spoke His Word to His people. In its various forms the word appears over 660 times in the Bible, two-thirds of which are in the Old Testament.

1. When the name "Israel" is used in this manual, it refers to the chosen nation as a whole, unless otherwise specified.

A. The Term "Prophesy"

The primary task of the Old Testament prophets was not to *foretell* future events but to *forthtell* the will of God which He had revealed to His prophets. Concerning the verb "prophesy," Gleason Archer writes:

> The Hebrew word is **nibba'** . . . a word whose etymology is much disputed. The best rounded explanation, however, seems to relate this root to the Akkadian verb **nabu**, which means "to summon, announce, call. . . ." Thus the verb **nibba'** would doubtless signify one who has been called or appointed to proclaim as a herald the message of God Himself. From this verb comes the characteristic word for prophet, **nabi'**, one who has been called. On this interpretation the prophet was . . . one called by God to proclaim as a herald from the court of heaven the message to be transmitted from God to man.[2]

B. Qualifications of the Prophet

Listed below are some of the qualifications for the high office of the prophet. Considering the nature of the prophet's work, we can appreciate why the qualifications were so strict:

1. SOVEREIGN CALLING
God's sovereign will determined who were His prophets (cf. Is 6; Jer 1).

2. SPECIAL ABILITIES
These were given by God's Spirit, enabling the prophet to perceive the truth (as "seer"), and equipping him with the gift of communicating to people the revelation of God.

3. SPIRITUAL QUALITIES
These were not a few. Included were unselfishness, obedience to the voice of God, love and faith, courage and long-suffering.

C. Message of the Prophet

Whether the prophet was called to preach, or to write, or to do both, his message was the same. All the prophetic words of the Old Testament could probably be compiled under the following four large areas of truth about which the prophet engaged himself:

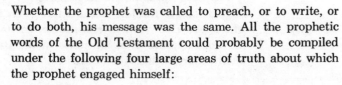

2. Gleason L. Archer, *A Survey of Old Testament Introduction*, p. 284.

1. INSTRUCTION OF THE GREAT TRUTHS
   ABOUT GOD AND MAN
The prophets devoted much time telling the people about God—His character, His domain, His purposes, and His law. They also gave a true diagnosis of the spiritual health of the nation as a whole and of the individual souls.

2. WARNING AND APPEAL TO THOSE LIVING IN SIN
It cannot be said that God brings judgment upon men without forewarning. Over and over again the prophets warned of judgment to come for sin, and exhorted the people to repent and turn to God.

3. COMFORT AND EXHORTATION TO THOSE
   TRUSTING AND OBEYING GOD
These are the warm and bright portions of the prophets' messages.

4. PREDICTION OF EVENTS TO COME
Prophetic predictions were of two major subjects: (1) national and international events, of both near and far-distant future; and (2) the coming of Jesus the Messiah— His first and second comings.

D. The Writing Prophets

There are seventeen books of prophecy in our English Old Testament. These were written by sixteen different prophets, if Jeremiah wrote Lamentations as well as the book bearing his name. The books are classified as either "Major" or "Minor," the classification assigned primarily for their relative length. These prophecies were written over a period of more than four centuries, from about 840 B.C. (Obadiah) to 420 B.C. (Malachi).

Writers of the Major Prophetical Books	Writers of the Minor Prophetical Books		
Isaiah	Hosea	Jonah	Zephaniah
Jeremiah	Joel	Micah	Haggai
Ezekiel	Amos	Nahum	Zechariah
Daniel	Obadiah	Habakkuk	Malachi

II. UNDERSTANDING THE PROPHETIC BOOKS

An Old Testament prophet's twofold ministry was that of *forthtelling* and *foretelling*. In order to understand both of these as they appear in the books of the minor prophets, you should be aquainted with the historical setting (where forthtelling is prominent) and with the times beyond the horizons (where foretelling is prominent).

A. The Historical Setting

Because history involves geography, it is important to know the locations of the major nations during the times of the prophets. Always have a mental picture of these as you study the prophets.

For each prophetic book there is both a large overall historical setting, and the immediate setting.

1. OVERALL SETTING

Israel was God's elect nation, called into being by His sovereign decree, and preserved through the ages (sometimes in a very small remnant) in fulfillment of His covenant originally made with Abraham (Gen 12).

MAJOR NATIONS DURING THE TIMES OF THE PROPHETS   Map 2

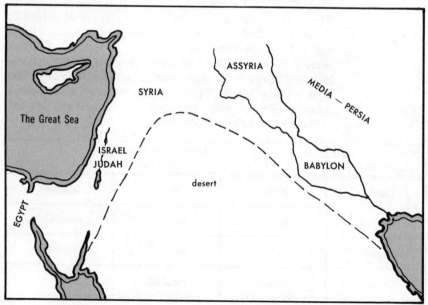

Refer to Chart A and note that all the writing prophets ministered subsequent to the split of the united kingdom into two kingdoms, Israel and Judah (931 B.C.).[3] At the close of Samuel's judgeship (c. 1000 B.C.), Israel had willfully insisted upon having human kings rule over them in spite of God's solemn protest and warning of the consequences of such a step. God gave them what they demanded, and over the years the kings exerted great power and influence. Many of them were wicked men, leading multitudes of the people into idolatry and all forms of disobedience to God. At such a time as this, God must speak. Although Israel had rejected God, He had not rejected Israel; and while their human kings were leading the people away from Him, God, through the voice of the prophets, was seeking to woo them back to Himself. This was the occasion for the introduction of the prophets. The prophet was God's mouthpiece, speaking His warnings and predictions and exhortations.

2. IMMEDIATE SETTING

One must also understand something of the political and religious conditions which prevailed at the time any given prophet was speaking. For most of the prophetic books, this can be ascertained by reading in the books of Kings and Chronicles the history of the kings who were ruling at any particular period. For example, the first verse of Micah gives the names of the three kings who were reigning while Micah was prophesying. By turning back to the historical books and reading the accounts of these reigns, one can learn about the evils which existed and against which Micah was thundering.

The setting of foreign powers also throws light on the prophetic books. For each book you will want to know something of the surrounding nations, especially those vying for world suzerainty. Chart A shows that the three reigning world powers during the years of the prophets were:

Assyrian—up to 612 B.C. (fall of Nineveh)
Neo-Babylonian—up to 539 B.C. (fall of Babylon)
Persian—up to Malachi (and beyond)

You will appreciate and understand more of the historical move of the prophets' days if you always keep in

3. This is an example of the smaller designation of the name Israel.

THE WRITING PROPHETS IN OLD TESTAMENT HISTORY

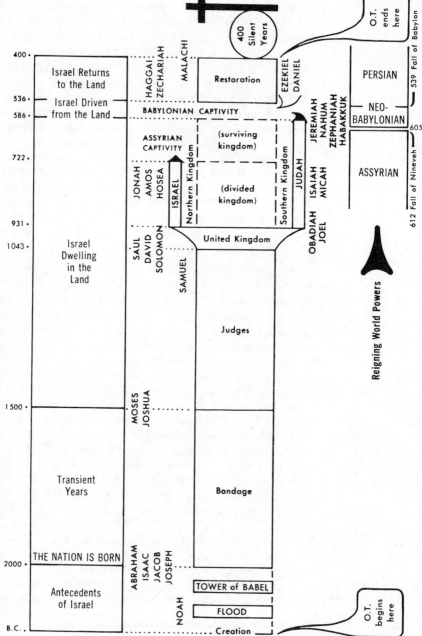

mind that human history is in the sovereign hands of an omniscient, omnipotent God. Everything transpires either by His permission or directive will. He foreknows every event before it becomes history, and on many occasions He gave such prophetic revelation to His prophets to share with the nations.

B. Beyond the Horizons

A vital and unique mission of the prophets was to foretell the future as God revealed it to them.

1. THE FOUR PROPHETIC POINTS

The utterances of the prophets, for the most part, centered around four points in history: (1) their own time; (2) the threatening captivities (Assyrian and Babylonian), and subsequent restoration; (3) the coming of their Messiah; and (4) the Messianic kingdom (sometimes called millennium) of the end times. This is illustrated by Chart B.

It was as though the prophet were on some high eminence (see "A" on Chart B) looking off into the distance and speaking of what he saw. Most often he saw the sins

FOUR PROPHETIC POINTS   **Chart B**

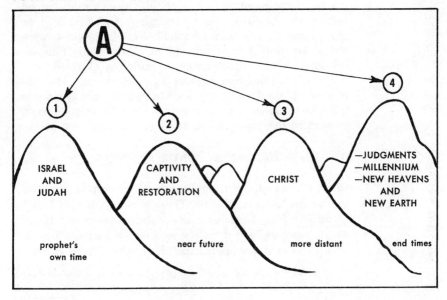

which prevailed in his own day, and spoke of them (see Pt. 1 on Chart B). Then he would look off to the day when the nation would be taken out of their fair land into captivity. He also saw an eventual regathering of the Jews from the captivities (see Pt. 2). At times the Spirit enabled him to look further into the future and foretell of the coming Messiah (see Pt. 3). Often he saw still further into the future and spoke of such things as restoration and peace coming to God's people in a glorious kingdom (see Pt. 4). As an example, read Micah 4 and determine to which of these four times of history Micah is referring.

Whenever a prophet foretells an event, you will want to determine which future category it is in (Pts. 2, 3, or 4 on Chart B). In making your interpretation, keep in mind that often a prophecy has a multiple intention of fulfillment. For example, a prophecy of restoration of the Jews may concern (1) return from Babylonian captivity *and also* (2) regathering of Israel from all parts of the world in the end times. Actually the restoration after the Babylonian captivity was so temporary and partial that all promises of a glorious restoration looked ultimately to the future Messianic reign, of end times.

2. THE TWO MESSIANIC THEMES

An Old Testament prophecy about Christ's ministry on earth concerns either His first coming (e.g., Mic 5:2) or His second coming (e.g., Mic 2:12-13). The prophets were not aware that a long interval of time would transpire between Christ's manifestation in suffering (first advent) and Christ's revelation in glory (second advent). His suffering and His reigning appeared to them to be very close in time. The student of prophecy must keep this in mind when he studies the predictive sections of the prophetic books.

III. THREE GROUPS OF MINOR PROPHETS

Chart C shows the three groups of minor prophets in relation to the historical setting. There were prophets of Israel (Northern Kingdom); prophets of Judah (Southern Kingdom); and prophets of the restored nation (after returning from exile).[4] According to the chart, what is the chrono-

4. These are the subjects, respectively, of the three books of this self-study series devoted to the minor prophets.

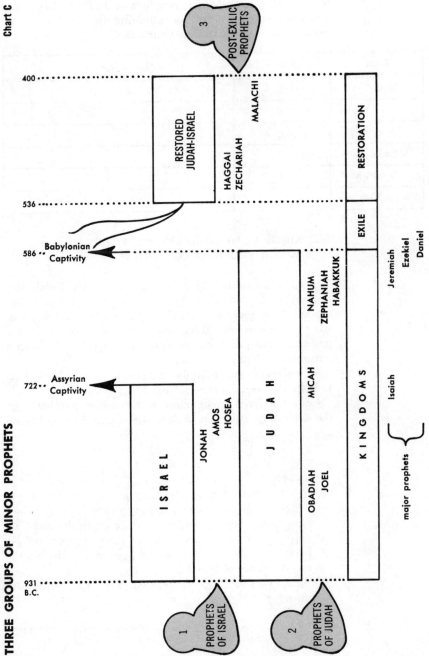

THREE GROUPS OF MINOR PROPHETS

Chart C

400 ·

3 POST-EXILIC PROPHETS

RESTORED JUDAH-ISRAEL

MALACHI

HAGGAI ZECHARIAH

RESTORATION

536 ·

Babylonian Captivity

EXILE

586 ·

NAHUM ZEPHANIAH HABAKKUK

Jeremiah
Ezekiel
Daniel

722 · · Assyrian Captivity

MICAH

Isaiah

J U D A H

ISRAEL

JONAH AMOS HOSEA

OBADIAH JOEL

K I N G D O M S

major prophets

931 ·
B.C.

1 PROPHETS OF ISRAEL

2 PROPHETS OF JUDAH

13

logical order of the minor prophets of Judah? This is the order in which we will be studying the books in this manual. Try to fix this in your mind:

BOOK	NO. OF CHAPTERS	NOTE
Obadiah	1	
Joel	3	
Micah	7	
Nahum	3	
Zephaniah	3	
Habakkuk	3	

IV. KINGS CONTEMPORARY WITH THE MINOR PROPHETS OF JUDAH

Chart D shows which kings were reigning over Judah during the ministries of Judah's six minor prophets.[5] The shaded areas indicate the evil reigns; the unshaded areas, the righteous reigns. What seems to have brought on the appearance of prophets: good, or evil reigns? Or is such a pattern not clear?

When you begin to study each book, refer to this chart to help you visualize the setting.

(Note: For more background on the minor prophets, see the self-study guide on *Jonah, Amos and Hosea*, Lesson 1.)

*   *   *

Review Questions

1. How many minor prophets ministered to Judah? Can you name them, in the order of their appearance?
2. How many prophets ministered primarily to the Northern Kingdom of Israel?
3. What prophets are associated with the post-exilic times?

---

5. Most of the dates are from John C. Whitcomb's *Chart of Kings and Prophets* (Moody Press).

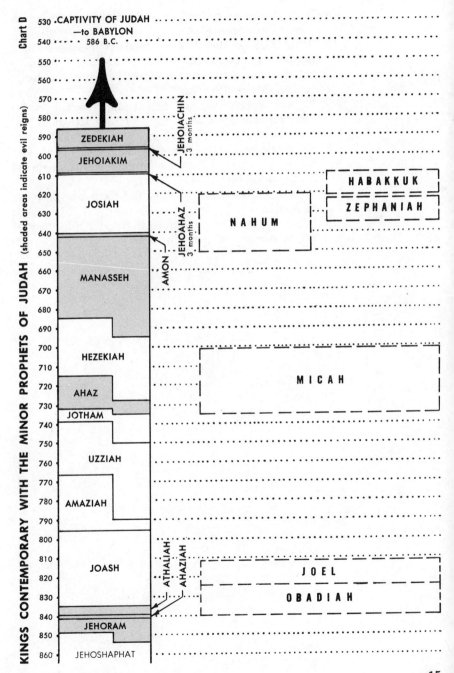

Chart D

KINGS CONTEMPORARY WITH THE MINOR PROPHETS OF JUDAH (shaded areas indicate evil reigns)

- 530 — CAPTIVITY OF JUDAH
- 540 — —to BABYLON 586 B.C.
- 550
- 560
- 570
- 580
- 590 — ZEDEKIAH
- 600 — JEHOIAKIM
- 610
- 620 — JOSIAH
- 630
- 640
- 650
- 660 — MANASSEH
- 670
- 680
- 690
- 700 — HEZEKIAH
- 710
- 720 — AHAZ
- 730 — JOTHAM
- 740
- 750
- 760 — UZZIAH
- 770
- 780 — AMAZIAH
- 790
- 800
- 810 — JOASH
- 820
- 830
- 840
- 850 — JEHORAM
- 860 — JEHOSHAPHAT

JEHOIACHIN 3 months

JEHOAHAZ 3 months

AMON

ATHALIAH

AHAZIAH

HABAKKUK

ZEPHANIAH

NAHUM

MICAH

JOEL

OBADIAH

4. In your own words, what was the main function of an Old Testament prophet?
5. What were the two different kinds of messages which the prophets delivered?
6. What is the intention of the word *minor* in the designation "Minor Prophets"?
7. Nahum, Zephaniah, and Habakkuk preached to the Southern Kingdom after the Northern Kingdom had gone into captivity in 722 B.C.—true or false?
8. Captivity, restoration, the first coming of Christ, and the return of Christ were all future events predicted by the prophets—true or false?
9. Which is the longest book of the six minor prophets of Judah?
10. Were evil kings on the throne during the ministries of *all* the minor prophets of Judah?

A Rock That Fails
and a Kingdom that Endures

SOME PROPHETS WERE COMMISSIONED

TO PREACH TO FOREIGN NATIONS

CLOSELY INVOLVED WITH JUDAH'S HISTORY.

Obadiah was God's messenger to Edom, the hostile kingdom southeast of Judah. (See Map 1.) The Gentile Edomites felt militarily secure in the fortresses of their steep mountains, and wanted nothing to do with Israel's God.

If any city of Edom was a symbol of arrogant self-confidence, it was Petra (Heb., *Sela*, 2 Ki 14:7). This now-famous tourist attraction of the red-rock canyons is located about fifty miles south of the Dead Sea. Obadiah may have had Petra in mind when he wrote in verse 3: "The pride of thine heart hath deceived thee, thou that dwellest in the clefts of the *rock* [Heb., *sela*; Gk., *petra*]."[1]

As you study Obadiah in this lesson, you will see how God was vitally interested in Gentiles as well as Jews in Old Testament times. The book's main spiritual lesson is that life's only sure foundation is God Himself.

I. BACKGROUND OF THE BOOK

A. The Man Obadiah

The name "Obadiah" appears twenty times in the Bible, representing thirteen different persons. The only reference to the writing prophet is in verse one of his book. His home was in Judah, and he lived probably during the reigns of Jehoram, Ahaziah, Athaliah and Joash (Chart

---

1. An alternative reading of this phrase is: "thou that dwellest in the clefts of Sela."

D).[2] The name *Obadiah* means "servant of the Lord" or "worshiper of the Lord."

B. The Book of Obadiah
1. DATE WRITTEN
There are a few possible dates. If we knew which plundering of Jerusalem Obadiah was referring back to in verses 11-14, we could be more certain of the book's date. (The book was written *later* than the plundering.) Read verses 11-14. Four invasions of Jerusalem are recorded in Old Testament history:

a) by Shishak, king of Egypt (925 B.C.). 1 Kings 14:25-26; 2 Chronicles 12

b) by Philistines and Arabians (during reign of Jehoram; see Chart D). 2 Chronicles 21:16-17; cf. 2 Chronicles 21:8-10; Amos 1:6, 11-12

c) by Jehoash, king of Israel (*c.* 790 B.C.). 2 Kings 14; 2 Chronicles 25

d) by Nebuchadnezzar, king of Babylon (586 B.C.). 2 Kings 24-25; cf. Psalm 137:7

Read the four groups of passages cited above. This manual takes the position that Obadiah, in verses 11-14, was referring to the plundering by Philistines and Arabians (second invasion cited above).[3] Based on this, his book was written between 840 and 825 B.C.

2. CONTENT AND STYLE
Obadiah is the shortest book of the Old Testament, but the familiar slogan *multum in parvo* ("much in little") certainly applies to it. Hugo of St. Victor described the book thus:

> Obadiah is simple in language, manifold in meaning; few in words, abundant in thoughts, according to that "the wise man is known by the fewness of his words." He directeth his prophecy, according to the letter, against Edom; allegorically he inveighs against the world; morally against the flesh. Bearing an image of the Saviour, he hinteth at His coming through whom the world is destroyed, through whom the flesh is subdued, through whom freedom is restored.[4]

2. This is based on the view of an early date of the book, discussed later in the lesson.
3. Read Hobart E. Freeman, *An Introduction to the Old Testament Prophets*, pp. 140-41, for reasons supporting this view. Many Bible students prefer the fourth view, which places Obadiah as the last of the minor prophets of Judah and a contemporary of Jeremiah. Consult various commentaries about this.
4. Quoted by Frank E. Gaebelein, *Four Minor Prophets*, p. 16.

The style of the book is vigorous and colorful, using many striking comparisons. It is a compact version of the typical prophetic book, where the opening chapters deal with sin and judgment, and bright Messianic prophecies appear toward the end. The tragic aspect of the book is that Edom as a nation has come to a spiritual "point of no return"—that is, she is not offered any hope of salvation. One writer says "she is the only neighbor of the Israelites who was not given any promise of mercy from God."[5] This is not because God was unmerciful. Edom had already spurned the mercies of God.

3. HISTORICAL BACKGROUND

Since the destiny of Edom is a key subject of this book, some highlights of that nation's history are listed below, to furnish setting for the prophecy. (Read all the Bible passages.)

a) Nation was descended from Esau (Gen 25:19-34).

b) Nation settled in the regions of Mt. Seir (between the Dead Sea and Gulf of Akaba, to the east of the Arabah; see Map 1, "Geography of the Minor Prophets of Judah." (Gen 36).

c) Nation rejected the Israelites' request to travel through Edom on the journey from Egypt (Num 20:14-21).

d) Antagonism originating with the twin brothers Jacob and Esau (Gen 27) persisted through the centuries involving Israel (Jacob) and Edom (Esau). (Recall the passages cited earlier in this lesson about the plundering of Jerusalem. Also read 2 Sa 8:14; 2 Ki 14:1-7; 2 Ch 28:17.)

e) Nation was continually subject to foreign kingdoms, losing its identity as a nation before the time of Christ, and finally disappearing from history in A.D. 70. (Romans' destruction of Jerusalem).

II. SURVEY OF THE BOOK

Read the twenty-one verses of Obadiah in one sitting, aloud if possible. What are your first impressions? In your own words, what is the book mainly about?

Chart E is a survey of the book, showing its structural organization. A survey chart may be likened to a map which shows the layout of a land. Use the chart while you

5. Clyde E. Harrington, "Edom," in *The Zondervan Pictorial Bible Dictionary*, ed. Merrill C. Tenney (Grand Rapids: Zondervan, 1963) p. 234.

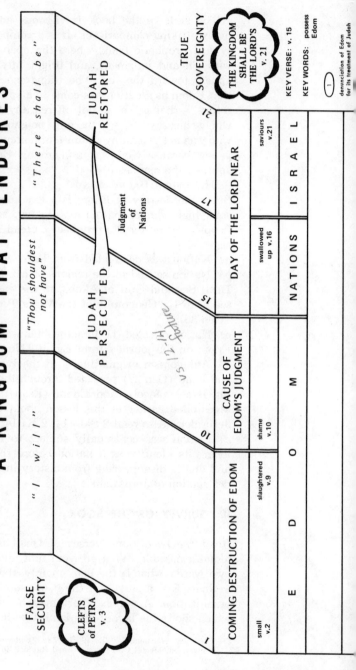

OBADIAH A ROCK THAT FAILS AND A KINGDOM THAT ENDURES

"I will" "Thou shouldest not have" "There shall be"

FALSE SECURITY

CLEFTS of PETRA v. 3

JUDAH PERSECUTED

vs 12-14 failure

JUDAH RESTORED

Judgment of Nations

TRUE SOVEREIGNTY

COMING DESTRUCTION OF EDOM		CAUSE OF EDOM'S JUDGMENT	DAY OF THE LORD NEAR	
1		10	15	17	21
small v.2	slaughtered v.9	shame v.10	swallowed up v.16	saviours v.21
E D O M			NATIONS	ISRAEL

THE KINGDOM SHALL BE THE LORD'S v.21

KEY VERSE: v. 15

KEY WORDS: possess Edom

① denunciation of Edom for its treatment of Judah

are analyzing the text later, just as a traveler uses his map. For now, note the following on the chart:

1. The book is of three main sections: verses 1-9; 10-14; and 15-21. Note the three different verb tenses shown at the top of the chart. Read the Bible text to see if these tenses are the prevailing ones of each section. (Note: The past tense of such verses as 2 and 7 in the first paragraph are more correctly represented as future tense.[6])

2. What part does Edom play in the book, according to the outlines shown? Check this out with the Bible text.

3. What part does Judah play in the book? (The reference to "Israel" in verse 20 is not to the northern kingdom exclusively, but to the chosen nation as a whole. This also is how the name "Israel" is used on the chart.)

4. Where is the bright section of the book?

5. Compare the beginning (v. 3) and the end (v. 21) of Obadiah. Relate to this the title shown at the top of the chart.

6. Note the outline of words beginning with the letter "s". Read the verses in the Bible text.

7. Note the key verses and key words. Add to the list of key words as you study the Bible text further.

8. Use the blank areas at the bottom of the chart to record observations and outlines of your own.

III. ANALYSIS

Paragraph divisions: at verses 1, 10, 15, 17. (Mark these in your Bible.)

A. Prophecy of Edom's Destruction: Vv. 1-9

What verses clearly tell who metes out the judgments?

_____

What are some of the descriptions given here of Edom's

judgments? _____

_____

6. Often a prophet worded a prediction in the past tense to give the emphasis of *sureness* of fulfillment.

Is anything said in this paragraph about the cause of the nation's judgments? _____

B. Cause of Edom's Judgment: Vv. 10-14
Verse 10 introduces the theme of the entire paragraph. What is the theme, in your own words? _____

_____

In what three ways are the Jews identified in this paragraph? (vv. 10, 12, 13) _____

_____

_____

What repeated phrase stands out in the paragraph? _____

_____

In what ways had Edom sinned against Judah? _____

_____

What is said here about Edom's coming judgment? _____

_____

C. Judgment of Gentile Nations: Vv. 15-16
What do the verses teach about these three holy things:
  holy day—"day of the LORD"
  holy principle—"As thou hast done, it shall be
    done unto thee"
  holy ground—"holy mountain"
  Does verse 16 suggest that Israel would be oppressed by other Gentile nations, as Edom had oppressed her?

D. Deliverance on Mt. Zion: Vv. 17-21
These concluding verses of Obadiah stress the bright hope of Israel in the Messianic kingdom, when the "day of the LORD" (v. 15) arrives.
  Ponder the significance of these three words of verse 17, as related to Judah:

"deliverance"
"holiness"
"possessions" (cf. Gen 15:18-21)
How does the phrase "possess their possessions" (v. 17) introduce the theme of the prophecies of verses 18-20?

What is the key repeated word of vv. 19-20? What is suggested by these verses concerning the role of Israel in the end times? _____

What has taken place in Palestine in the last few decades to set the stage for those times? _____

The first half of verse 21 summarizes the book's message about Judah (Zion) and Edom (Esau). State this in your own words. _____

The climactic words of the books are the last ones: "And the kingdom shall be the LORD's." This is the final word of all prophecy. Read these verses which reflect the same truth: Psalm 22:28; 103:19; Luke 1:33. Why was it important for Judah to be reminded of this key truth? (See

Notes.) _____
Note that the prophecy of salvation is identified with Jerusalem ("Mt. Zion") in verses 17 and 21. Read Luke 2:38, which says that just before Jesus was born many people "looked for redemption in Jerusalem." Whom did Simeon (Lk 2:25-35) and Anna (Lk 2:36-39) recognize as the world's Redeemer? _____

IV. NOTES

1. "Edom" (v. 1). The name means literally "red." Read Genesis 25:25-30; 36:8-9.

2. "Wise men out of Edom" (v. 8). The city of Teman (v. 9) was especially noted for its wise men (Jer 49:7). Eliphaz, one of Job's three friends, was a native of Teman (Job 2:11). Do you think Edom's pride (v. 3) may have involved vanity over intellectual superiority?

3. "The house of Jacob shall possess their possessions" (v. 17). That Israel has retained its identity for thousands of years is a miracle in itself. One day Israel shall worship Jesus as their Messiah (Ro 11:25-27). Now their eyes look only to the land, as expressed in their national anthem, *Hatikvah*:

> So long as still within our breasts
> The Jewish heart beats true,
> So long as still towards the East,
> To Zion, looks the Jew,
> So long our hopes are not yet lost—
> Two thousand years we cherished them—
> To live in freedom in the Land
> Of Zion and Jerusalem.

4. "The south" (v. 19). This was Negev, the desert region south of Judah.

5. "Sepharad (v. 20). Archer associates this place with a district called Shaparda in southwestern Media, mentioned in an inscription of King Sargon of Assyria.[7] (Cf. 2 Ki 18:11.)

6. "The kingdom shall be the LORD's" (v. 21). These words served more than one purpose in the book. "The danger which ever beset Israel was that of using prophecies such as Obadiah's to foster a spirit of vengefulness or to bolster up the hope of political or material expansion for the nation."[8]

V. FOR THOUGHT AND DISCUSSION

1. In what ways do people today practice the sin of arrogant independence of God?

2. Compare the two types of people suggested by this listing:

7. Gleason L. Archer, *A Survey of Old Testament Introduction*, pp. 289-90.
8. *The Westminster Study Edition of the Holy Bible* (Philadelphia: Westminster, 1948), p. 1310.

brothers:	ESAU	JACOB
nations:	Edom	Israel
citizenship:	earthly	heavenly
character:	proud, rebellious	chosen, set apart

3. What does the Bible teach about the consequences which fall upon the nation which oppresses His chosen people? Does Genesis 12:3 apply to today, and to end times?

4. "Does justice triumph?" This question has been asked by people throughout the ages. Does the book of Obadiah give any answers?

5. God's "mercy endureth for ever" (Ps 106:1). Why do some people see a conflict between this truth and the fact of eternal judgment?

6. Compare these verses which state the eternal law of returns:

"As thou hast done, it shall be done unto thee" (Ob 15).

"With what measure ye mete, it shall be measured to you again" (Mt 7:2).

"Whatsoever a man soweth, that shall he also reap" (Gal 6:7).

7. What Christian hymns come to your mind which magnify Christ as the believer's rock or foundation? Reflect on the precious truths taught in such hymns.

VI. FURTHER STUDY

Compare these other passages which record prophecies concerning Edom:

Numbers 24:18-19 Ezekiel 35:1-15
Isaiah 34:5-17; 63:1-6 Joel 3:19
Jeremiah 49:7-22 Amos 1:11-12
Lamentations 4:21-22

*   *   *

IN CONCLUSION

He is the Stone that some will stumble over, and the Rock
that will make them fall. They will stumble because they will
not listen to God's Word, nor obey it (1 Pe 2:8, TLB).
He is very precious to you who believe (1 Pe 2:7a, TLB).

On Christ, the solid Rock, I stand;
All other ground is sinking sand.
Edward Mote

JOEL 800 BC

declare judgements of God & exhort
to observe them   1-7

to mourn   8-13

fast to have deliverance from
        judgements   14-20

The day of the Lord will come

locusts

Background and Survey of Joel

JOEL WAS THE PROPHET WHO FOCUSED

HIS MESSAGE PRIMARILY ON THE GREAT

AND TERRIBLE DAY OF THE LORD.

His book of three chapters is a clear and strong presentation of the world-history view which sees all history culminating in Christ, and Israel as a prominent participant in end-times events.

This lesson studies the background of the book's writing and then makes a general survey of its contents. If you are studying in a group you will probably want to divide the lesson into at least two study units.

I. BACKGROUND OF THE BOOK

R. A. Stewart calls Joel "one of the most disturbing and heart-searching books of the Old Testament."[1] Let us look at the setting in which such a book originated. (First scan the book quickly before studying the background.)

A. The Man Joel

Very little is known of this prophet. According to 1:1, Joel ("Jehovah is God") was the son of Pethuel ("persuaded of God"). This is the only appearance of Pethuel in the Bible. The name Joel was very common in Old Testament times. This is borne out by the fact that there are about a dozen persons in the Bible with the name.

Joel lived in Judah, possibly Jerusalem, during the reign of King Joash. (See Chart D.) Some think that he was a priest when God called him to be a prophet.[2] Obadiah

---

1. R. A. Stewart, "Joel," in *The New Bible Dictionary*, ed. J. D. Douglas, p. 639.
2. Recall that Jeremiah was a priest when he received the prophet's call (Jer. 1:1-2).

was Judah's prophet just before Joel appeared on the scene.

B. The Book of Joel

1. DATE WRITTEN

If Joel lived during the reign of Joash, he was one of the earliest writing prophets. The book then was written around 820 B.C. (Chart D). Some Bible students prefer the view that Joel lived after the Babylonian exile (586 B.C.).[3] This manual follows the view of the early date.

2. SETTING

a) Political and religious. Joash[4] was king of Judah when Joel ministered as the nation's prophet. He began his forty-year reign when he was only seven years old, and his guardian-instructor in the early years was the godly high priest Jehoiada.[5] Up until Jehoiada's death, Joash's reign was mainly a righteous one (2 Ki 12:2). When Jehoiada died, Joash defected to idolatrous ways, even slaying Jehoiada's godly son. (Read 2 Chron 24:15-25.) Joel probably wrote his book while Joash was still a minor under Jehoiada's tutelage. This may partly account for the absence in Joel of long descriptions of national sin, usually found in the messages of the prophets.

During Joash's reign Judah was not free from the threat of invasion by foreigners. Read 2 Kings 12:17-19 and 2 Chronicles 24:23-25 which describe the Syrian invasion toward the end of Joash's life.

b) Economic. Severe plagues of locusts and draught had recently devastated the land of Judah when Joel penned his prophecy. In the opening lines of the book he asks the elders,

> "Has anything like this happened in your days or in your fathers' days?" (1:2, NASB).

He is referring to the locust plagues, described in the next verse:

3. Refer to a commentary for a discussion of the different views on date. Among the authors favoring the early date are Gleason L. Archer, *A Survey of Old Testament Introduction*, pp. 292-95, and J. T. Carson in *The New Bible Commentary*, pp. 690-91.
4. Joash is the shortened form of Jehoash. Both names appear in the Bible, referring to the same king.
5. This story of Joash and Jehoiada is reported in 2 Ki 11-12. Read these chapters to get a feel of the times in which Joel lived.

> "What the gnawing locust has left, the swarming locust has
>   eaten;
> And what the swarming locust has left, the creeping locust
>   has eaten;
> And what the creeping locust has left, the stripping locust
>   has eaten" (1:4, NASB).[6]

Only those who have witnessed a locust plague can fully
appreciate why it is so dreaded. Here are some selected
firsthand descriptions by witnesses:[7]

> For the space of ten miles on each side of the Sea-Cow river
> and eighty or ninety miles in length. . . the whole surface
> might literally be said to be covered with them [South Africa].

> When they approached our garden all the farm servants were
> employed to keep them off, but to no avail; though our men
> broke their ranks for a moment, no sooner had they passed the
> men, than they closed again, and marched forward through
> hedges and ditches as before. . . . They devour first grass and
> leaves, fruit and foliage, everything that is green and juicy.
> Then they attack the young branches of trees, and then the
> hard bark of the trunks. . . . The fields finished, they invade
> towns and houses, in search of stores. Victual of all kinds, hay,
> straw, and even linen and woolen clothes and leather bottles,
> they consume or tear in pieces [Syria].

Joel could not have used a better symbol than the locust
plague to prefigure the coming "terrible day of the LORD."

3. STYLE
The smooth and vivid style of Joel has contributed to his
book being called one of the literary gems of the Old Testament. Here are commendations by two authors:[8]

> There are other Prophets who write with greater passion and
> greater power, who rise to loftier altitudes of divine revelation;
> but there is hardly a writer in the Old Testament who shows
> proof of so careful, and detailed, and exquisite pains to give
> his work literary polish, finish and beauty.
>   W. G. Elmslie

> With the strength of Micah, it combines the tenderness of Jere-
> miah, the vividness of Nahum, and the sublimity of Isaiah.
>   A. R. Fausset

6. Derward Deere says these were four of the 80 or 90 species of locusts
    in the East (*The Wycliffe Bible Commentary*, p. 821).
7. Quoted by George Adam Smith, *The Book of the Twelve Prophets* (New
    York: Harper, n.d.), 2:392-95. See *The Zondervan Pictorial Bible Dic-
    tionary*, p. 377, for photos showing what a 15-minute locust attack has
    done to a tree.
8. Quoted in *The New Bible Commentary*, p. 690.

4. Purposes

Three main purposes of Joel's prophecy are: (1) to foretell coming judgments upon Judah for their sin; (2) to exhort Judah to turn their hearts to the Lord; and (3) to impress upon all people that this world's history will culminate in the events of the Day of the Lord, when the scales of justice will finally rest.

5. The Day of the Lord

Five times in Joel the phrase "the day of the Lord" appears. As we shall see in the next lesson, Joel is looking with his prophetic telescope to the end of time. Even when the New Testament writers referred to that day, it was still future. For example, read 2 Thessalonians 2:2 and 2 Peter 3:10. In the Old Testament the phrase occurs over thirty times, in such verses as Isaiah 2:12; 13:6, 9; Joel 1:15; Amos 5:18, Ezekiel 13:5; 30:3; Zephaniah 1:7, 14. Read these passages, observing that the descriptions of this "day" are usually about judgment and war against sinners, a necessary purge before righteousness can reign. Saints are involved in this day in the sense that when the Lord brings judgment upon unbelievers, the saints are associated with their Lord in the victory. (For example, the Millennium, issuing out of the Battle of Armageddon, may be considered a part of this "day of the Lord." In this connection it should be observed that it will be during the Millennium that the many Old Testament promises to Israel will be fulfilled. Thus the Millennium is especially Israel-oriented.)

There are various views as to what period of time "the day of the Lord" refers to. The day's inception is usually seen at one of these times:

a) at the rapture when the Tribulation period begins[9]

b) shortly after the rapture, during the Tribulation

c) at the revelation (Christ's return to this earth after the Tribulation) when Christ defeats His foes at the Battle of Armageddon (cf. Rev 16:16)

You will want to come to your own conclusions concerning this identification. Refer to commentaries for help. The view pursued in this manual is the third one noted above.

---

9. See J. Dwight Pentecost, *Things to Come* (Grand Rapids: Dunham, 1958), pp. 229-31, for a description of this view.

A similar phrase, "day of Christ," appears in the New Testament at Philippians 1:10 and 2:16. (Compare also the corresponding phrases in these verses: 1 Co 1:8; 5:5; 2 Co 1:14; Phil 1:6.) This day will be inaugurated at the rapture of the saints. Merrill F. Unger compares "Day of the Lord" and "Day of Christ" thus:

> Day of the Lord is the protracted period commencing with the Second Advent of Christ [second phase of Christ's return] in glory and ending with the cleansing of the heavens and the earth by fire preparatory to the new heavens and the new earth of the eternal state (Is 65:17-19; 66:22; 2 Pe 3:13; Rev 21:1). The Day of the Lord as a visible manifestation of Christ upon the earth is to be distinguished from the Day of Christ. The latter is connected with the glorification of the saints and their reward in the heavenlies previous to their return with Christ to inaugurate the Day of the Lord. The Day of the Lord thus comprehends specifically the closing phases of the Tribulation and extends through the Millennial Kingdom. Apocalyptic judgments (Rev 4:1—19:6) precede and introduce the Day of the Lord.[10]

These distinctions are shown on Chart F. The Battle of

TWO PROPHETIC DAYS

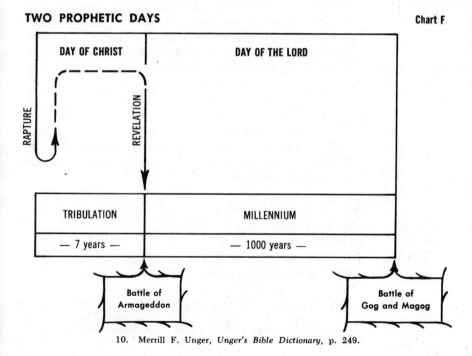

10. Merrill F. Unger, *Unger's Bible Dictionary*, p. 249.

Armageddon is the climactic event of judgment of the tribulation period which inaugurates the Day of the Lord. Thus the day of Christ begins at the rapture, and the Day of the Lord begins at the revelation.

To summarize, prophecies of the Day of the Lord are about the Messianic kingdom at the end of the world, which will begin when God's final judgment will fall upon unbelieving nations, and when believing Israel will be delivered from their enemies.

II. SURVEY OF THE BOOK OF JOEL

Survey study should always precede analysis of the Bible text. ("Image the whole, then execute the parts.") Spend the first ten minutes of your survey reading the three chapters in one sitting. What are your first impressions? What words and phrases especially stand out as prominent ones?

Imagine yourself as a Jewish farmer living in the days of Joel, not much concerned about spiritual things, a believer in God but not walking in fellowship with Him. How might you react to reading Joel's book for the first time?

Chart G is a survey chart of Joel, showing its overall structure. Study the chart very carefully at this time. Observe the following entries on the chart, referring to the Bible text to justify their inclusion on the chart:[11]

1. The first verse is the book's introduction. Is there a similar concluding verse?

 # 7

2. The book is of two main parts (1:2—2:11 and 2:28—3:21), with a bright section of exhortation sandwiched in between (2:12-27). At what point in the book does Joel look beyond the time of Christ (A.D.)?

3. Notice the sequence shown on the chart: locusts—Lord's army—signs—war—restoration. Scan the passages in your Bible to see the basis for this outline.

4. Study the other outlines shown below the base line. Is there an overall progression in the theme?

11. This is an example of deductive study in which you are told what the Bible says, and then you check to see if this is so. The opposite approach is inductive study in which you look at the Bible text first and then arrive at your own survey chart. Try making your own chart sometime.

Chart G

JOEL THE DAY OF THE LORD

DESCRIPTIONS AND PROPHECIES POINTING TO THE DAY OF THE LORD

1:15   2:1   2:11   DAY OF THE LORD   2:31   3:14   (3:18)

NOW, MOURNING OVER DESOLATION

THEN, REJOICING OVER DELIVERANCE

1:1 introduction	2:1	2:12	CALL TO REPENTANCE	2:28	DAY OF THE LORD 3:16b	blessing on Israel (millennium) 3:21
					judgment on nations	

locusts   Lord's army (2:11)   signs-war-restoration

J U D A H		GENTILE NATIONS & ISRAEL	
awful plague now	worse coming	RESTORATION POSSIBLE	Spirit era	Finally, the DAY OF THE LORD
①	②	exhortation	③	④
PRESENT	IMMINENT	CONDITIONAL FUTURE	DISTANT	U L T I M A T E

B. C.   **A. D.**

KEY WORDS:
locust
day of the Lord (5x)
rejoicing
restore

KEY VERSES:
2:21, 32a

OUTSTANDING PASSAGES:
2:1-11
2:28-32
3:18-21

33

5. Note where the five references to "the day of the LORD" appear in the book. Read each reference in your Bible.

6. What two aspects of "the day of the LORD" appear in the two parts of 2:30—3:21?

7. Compare the beginning of the book ("now") with the ending ("then").

8. Read the key verses in your Bible. Note the list of key words. Add to this list as you continue your study of the book.

9. You will want to refer back to this survey chart often during your analytical study in the next lesson.

*   *   *

Review Questions

1. What does the name *Joel* mean literally?

2. Who was king of Judah when Joel wrote his book? Describe his reign.

3. What were the economic circumstances of Judah in Joel's time?

4. What are three main purposes of the book of Joel?

5. What does the Bible teach about the Day of the Lord? What does Joel write about it in his book?

6. What subject first appears in the book? What subjects follow, to the end of the book?

7. How would you identify the three main sections of Joel, as to general content?

8. What is the concluding subject of the book?

9. Does Joel teach that Israel will be a prominent participant in world history in the last times? If so, what does he say about it?

10. What are some key words and phrases of the book?

34

The Day of the Lord Will Come!

IN THIS LESSON WE WILL WANT TO

CONCENTRATE OUR STUDY ON THE

SMALLER DETAILS OF JOEL'S PROPHECY.

This should prove to be a very interesting experience, for many unique phrases appear in the book (e.g., "multitudes in the valley of decision," 3:14). We will especially want to observe the contexts of the five appearances of the key phrase, "the day of the LORD." As we saw in Lesson 3, Joel's prophecy is summed up in the warning that *the Day of the Lord will surely come.*

I. PREPARATION FOR STUDY

The best preparation for this lesson is to review the background and survey studies of Lesson 3. For those studying

JOEL 1:1—2:11   Chart H

1:1	1:2		2:1		
	locusts	→	Lord's army		
	awful plague		worse judgment		
	PRESENT		**IMMINENT**		
INTRODUCTION		1:13		2:3	2:11

35

in a group, a large reproduction of the survey Chart G would greatly aid the discussion if it is kept in view at all times. Chart H is an excerpt of that survey chart.

II. ANALYSIS

Segments to be analyzed: 1:1—2:11; 2:12-27; and 2:28—3:21. (These are the three main sections of Chart G.)
Paragraph divisions: at verses 1:1, 2, 4, 8, 13; 2:1, 3, 12, 18, 21, 28, 30; 3:1, 4, 9, 16*b*.
The first verse of Joel tells us the source of the prophecy. What dimension does this add to the prophet's message?

_____

_____

A. Locust Judgments: 1:2—2:11

Read the descriptions of the locust plague in 1:4-12. (Use the NASB translation of 1:4 given in Lesson 3.) What affected groups of people are cited in verses 5, 9, 11, and 12? _____

_____

What verbs like "howl" (1:5) appear in the passage? _____

What do the last ten words of 1:12 tell you about Judah at this time? _____

_____

Now read 1:13-20. How is the Lord involved in the plague, according to these verses? _____

_____

What are the commands of verses 14-15? _____

How would similar commands be worded in the contemporary setting of the twentieth century? _____

_____

Relate verse 19*a* to the commands. _____

_____

In your own words, record the content of 1:2-12 and 1:13-20 in the two respective blank spaces of Chart H.
Read 2:1-11. Here Joel describes an invasion by either locusts or a military army. (Cf. 2:7, 11, 20, 25.) What do
you think is the invader?[1] _____
How does the judgment differ from that of chapter 1 as
to time and intensity? _____
What is taught about the Lord in the opening verses (1-2)
and closing verse (11)? _____

_____

What do the intervening verses (3-10) describe? Record these observations in the blank spaces of Chart H.
What does the concluding question of 2:11 emphasize?

(Translate "abide" as "endure.") _____

_____

What do you think is intended by the word "great" in the statement, "the day of the LORD is great and very terrible"

(2:11)? _____

_____

Was the invasion by locusts or armies the *climactic* judgment for Judah? If not, would it be correct to say that "the day of the LORD" as applied to that invasion *prefigured* the ultimate Day of Judgment, coming in the end times? Why did God have Joel preach the message of 1:2—2:11 (awful

plague now; worse coming)? _____

_____

B. Call to Repentance: 2:12-27

Read this passage, underlining key words and phrases as you read. Mark in your Bible the blocks of verses which record the Lord as speaking (12, 19-20, 25-27).

---

1. Most commentators interpret the invader as locusts. See Hobart E. Freeman, *An Introduction to the Old Testament Prophets*, pp. 152-54, for arguments favoring the military army view.

Write a list of all the things taught about repentance in 2:12-17. _____

_____

Record on the accompanying work sheet what is taught in each of the three paragraphs of this segment. For example, what is taught about God?

JOEL			
2:12	**2:18**	**2:21**	**2:27**
REPENTANCE	**RESTORATION**		
Now	Then		

Relate 2:25 to 1:4. Also compare 2:26 with 1:11.
Why is this central passage (2:12-27) the key of Joel's preaching? (See Chart G again.) _____

C. The Holy-Spirit Era to the End of Time: 2:28—3:21

Chart I is a work sheet for recording your observations as you study this important passage of Joel. Scan the chart and note how the text proceeds, topicwise, from verse to verse, beginning at 2:28 and concluding with 3:21. According to the chart, this is the pattern of Joel's discourse:

1. First, 2:28-29 is about the church age beginning with the Christians at Pentecost. (Read Acts 2:5-18.)[2]

2. This is a clear illustration of the principle of prophetic latitude whereby the prophet skips over centuries of time and casually predicts the next events as though they were nearby (e.g., "afterward," 2:28).

JOEL 2:28–3:21

Chart I

CHURCH AGE

2:28 afterward . . .

my spirit

my spirit

2:29

END TIMES CLIMAXING IN THE DAY OF THE LORD

JUDGMENT ON UNBELIEVING NATIONS

2:30

And [later] . . . WONDERS
. . . pillars of smoke

2:31

3:1

judgements on unbelieving ~~Israel~~ nations

3:4

3:9 war

heavens and the earth shall shake

3:16*a*

BLESSING ON BELIEVING ISRAEL

2:32

in Jerusalem shall be deliverance

3:16*b*

blessing on believing Israel

3:21

2. Then, 2:30-32 is a condensed version of the two aspects of the Day of the Lord:

a) judgments preceding the day (2:30-31)

b) deliverance for believing Israel (2:32). (Read Ro 10:13, where Paul quotes the first part of this verse in the "Israel section" of Romans.)

3. Finally, chapter 3 amplifies the descriptions of the two aspects of that day:

a) judgments on the unbelieving nations (3:1-16*a*)

b) blessing forever on believing Israel (3:16*b*-21)

Recall from your study of Lesson 3 how the two aspects of the Day of the Lord were shown on Chart F. Read Joel 2:28—3:21 again, and try to visualize the fulfillments of Joel's prophecies and the end times. Use Chart I especially to record key words and phrases of the passage.

What will be the cause for world judgments in the end

times? _____

_____

What will be the basis for the Jews' deliverance? _____

_____

III. NOTES

1. "The day of the Lord is great and very terrible" (2:11). Use an exhaustive concordance to see the many uses of the Hebrew word translated "great" in this verse. Some passages to read are Job 22:5; Psalm 48:1; 95:3; 136:17; 145:8; Jeremiah 21:5.

2. "Now" (2:12). *The Living Bible* adds this phrase for emphasis: "while there is time." Record this in your Bible. The time reference is a key ingredient of the experience of repentance.

3. "And I will shew wonders" (2:30). Read this as though the word "later" appears between the first two words. This is justified in view of the time reference at the end of verse 31: "before the . . . day . . . come." (For New Testament verses about signs referred to in Joel 2:30-31, see Mt 24:29 and Rev 6:12.)

4. "When I shall bring again the captivity of Judah" (3:1). The New American Standard Bible correctly translates, "When I restore the fortunes of Judah."

5. "Valley of Jehoshaphat" (3:2). The name "Jehoshaphat" means "Jehovah judges." Joel may be using the term "valley of Jehoshaphat" figuratively, to symbolize divine judgment (cf. "valley of decision" in 3:14). Some think the Valley of Jehoshaphat is the Kidron Valley, between Jerusalem and the Mount of Olives.

6. "Valley of decision" (3:14). This is not a reference to decision by man, for judgment day has already arrived as of this time. Rather, it is God's decision, or verdict, of the unbeliever's judgment. This valley, therefore, may be the same as the Valley of Jehoshaphat.

IV. FOR THOUGHT AND DISCUSSION

1. Are any or all of God's judgments only for purposes of punishment?

2. In what sense is God sovereign in all of His judgments? Can man's repentance change God's pronouncement of judgment? In answering this, see Jeremiah 18:7-10. When is a judgment of God irreversible?

3. "I will restore to you. . ." (2:25). Is God still in the "business" of restoration? Justify your answer.

4. What are the important ministries of the Holy Spirit today?

5. In what ways has Israel been persecuted by Gentiles since the days of Joel? Who has preserved a remnant of believing Jews through the centuries?

6. What spiritual lessons are taught by Joel which can be applied to today?

V. FURTHER STUDY

1. Study what the New Testament teaches about the judgment of nations in the last days. For example, see Matthew 25:31-46[3] and Revelation 19:11-21.

3. Some interpret this passage as referring to individual Gentiles, not nations as such. (The Greek word translated "nations" means literally "Gentiles.")

2. Compare the ministries of the Holy Spirit before and after the day of Pentecost.

*　　*　　*

A CONCLUDING THOUGHT

Multitudes, multitudes waiting in the valley for the verdict of their doom! (3:14, TLB).

Background and Survey of Micah

MICAH IS THE PROPHET USUALLY QUOTED

AT CHRISTMASTIME FOR PROPHESYING

THE CITY OF JESUS' BIRTH, BETHLEHEM.

Micah lived about the time of Isaiah, and there may have been a very close personal relation between the two prophets. So it is interesting to observe that today we associate Micah with the prophecy of Jesus' birth whereas Isaiah is often remembered for the stirring chapter about Jesus' death (chap. 53). Of course both prophets wrote about other truths as well.

I. BACKGROUND OF THE BOOK

The more we can see and feel the setting of Micah's message, the better we will be able to apply it to today. This is the purpose of the orientations and introductions that follow. Before reading the background material, make a quick scanning of the entire book of Micah.

A. The Man Micah

1. NAME
The name *Micah* means "Who is Jehovah like?" or "Who is like unto Jehovah?" Read the first words of 7:18. Do you think the prophet may have been thinking of his own name when he penned those words?

2. HOME
Micah's hometown was Moresheth-gath (1:1, 14), located about twenty miles southwest of Jerusalem. (See map.) The name Moresheth-gath means "possession of Gath," which suggests that the town was an annex of nearby Gath. The busy highway from Egypt to Jerusalem went through this area, so the "country boy" Micah was not too far removed from the city ways of his contemporary Isaiah.

↑ see p 66 for continuation ↑

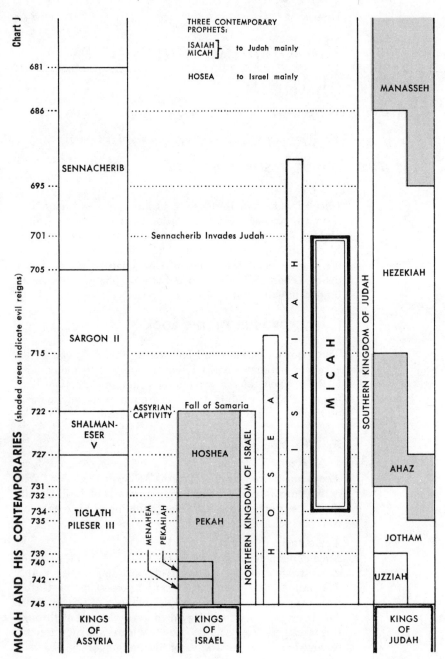

Chart J

MICAH AND HIS CONTEMPORARIES (shaded areas indicate evil reigns)

THREE CONTEMPORARY PROPHETS:

ISAIAH ⎱
MICAH ⎰ to Judah mainly

HOSEA   to Israel mainly

681 ···

686 ···

695 ···

701 ··· ···· Sennacherib Invades Judah ····

705 ···

715 ···

722 ···

727 ···

731 ···
732 ···

734 ···
735 ···

739 ···
740 ···

742 ···

745 ···

SENNACHERIB

SARGON II

SHALMAN-
ESER
V

TIGLATH
PILESER III

KINGS
OF
ASSYRIA

ASSYRIAN
CAPTIVITY

MENAHEM
PEKAHIAH

Fall of Samaria

HOSHEA

PEKAH

KINGS
OF
ISRAEL

NORTHERN KINGDOM OF ISRAEL

H O S E A

I S A I A H

M I C A H

SOUTHERN KINGDOM OF JUDAH

MANASSEH

HEZEKIAH

AHAZ

JOTHAM

UZZIAH

KINGS
OF
JUDAH

44

3. TIME

Study Chart J, which shows the contemporaries (kings and prophets) of Micah.

Answer the following on the basis of the chart:

a) Between what years did Micah minister as a prophet?

_____

b) What two other prophets ministered during Micah's

time? _____

c) Who were Judah's kings when Micah was prophesying?

_____

d) What calamity befell the Northern Kingdom of Israel

in the middle of Micah's ministry? _____

_____

e) Read Micah 1:5-7. (Samaria was the capital of Israel, just as Jerusalem was the capital of Judah.) Did Micah write these verses before or after the Assyrian captivity of

722 B.C.? _____

4. MINISTRY

Micah was a prophet mainly to Judah, though his messages did involve Israel (cf. 1:1; 3:8). He had a clear conviction as to his prophetic calling (3:8). His messages were directed to various evils: moral corruption, idolatry (1:7; 6:16), formal religion, corrupt leadership by false prophets (3:5-7) and by priests (3:11). There was social decay, with the rulers and wealthy people oppressing the poor (2:2; 3:1-3). There was a haunting political unrest, especially over fear of invasion by foreign powers. (See Is 7-12.) How Micah addressed these conditions will be seen when the Bible text is analyzed.

5. POLITICAL SETTING

To learn about the political setting of Micah, read 2 Kings 15:17—20:21 and 2 Chronicles 26-30. (Chronicles reports mainly about the Southern Kingdom.) Refer to Chart J as you read these historical sections, to see when each king reigned.

King Uzziah's reign was a successful one, but toward the end of his life he strayed far from God (2 Ch 26:16-23).

His son Jotham, who succeeded him, "did that which was right in the sight of the LORD" (2 Ch 27:2). Although he was not able to lead the people out of their corrupt ways, Jotham apparently supported Micah's spiritual program. But when, at his death, his son Ahaz mounted the throne, affairs took a different turn.

During Jotham's reign, clouds had begun to gather on the political horizon in the shape of a military coalition of Syria and Israel against Judah (2 Ki 15:37). When Ahaz became king of Judah, instead of searching out and dealing with the national sins for which God was allowing this chastisement, he formed an alliance with Tiglath Pileser, king of Assyria, an alliance which in the days of his son Hezekiah would prove almost fatal to the kingdom. He also introduced idolatry, with all its attendant evils, and even caused God's holy altar to be set aside, and one of heathen design put in its place (2 Ch 28:22-25).

King Hezekiah, who succeeded Ahaz, honored Jehovah in his administration of the kingdom. But such leadership and example brought only a measure of obedience on the part of the people. Though the outward form and ceremony of temple worship was kept up, all manner of sins were being committed by the people—sins of idolatry, covetousness, impurity, injustice, and oppression. Against all this the prophet's voice needed to be lifted. Micah and Isaiah were God's spokesmen for such a time as this.

B. The Book of Micah

The content and style of Micah's book reveal that he was a very gifted and knowledgeable servant of God. Let us look at some of the book's characteristics.

1. DATE WRITTEN
A probable date of writing is after the Assyrian conquest of Damascus (734-32 B.C.—2 Ki 16:5 ff.; Is 7-10), and before the fall of Samaria (722 B.C.—2 Ki 17).

2. MAIN THEME
The main theme which runs through the book of Micah is that God will send judgment for Judah's sin, but pardon is still offered. The message underscores the two divine attributes cited in Romans 11:22a: "Behold therefore the goodness and severity of God."

＃7 3. PROPHECIES NOW FULFILLED
Six specific prophecies of Micah have become events of
history. They are:
a) fall of Samaria, 722 B.C. (1:6-7)
b) invasion of Judah by Sennacherib, 702-701 B.C. (1:9-16)
c) fall of Jerusalem, 586 B.C. (3:12; 7:13)
d) exile in Babylon, 586 B.C. (4:10)
e) return from captivity, *c.* 520 B.C. (4:1-8, 13; 7:11, 14-17)
f) birth of Jesus in Bethlehem (5:2)

4. LITERARY FORMS
Word pictures abound in the book. Contrasts are prominent
(e.g., 3:9-12 and 4:1-5), and questions appear often (1:5;
2:7; 4:9; 6:3, 7, 10, 11; 7:10, 18). Compare the first question (1:5) and the last (7:18).

5. QUOTED IN THE BIBLE
Micah is quoted three times in the Bible. Each occasion is
significant. Read the passages:
a) elders of Judah, quoting Micah 3:12 in Jeremiah 26:18
b) magi, quoting Micah 5:2 in Matthew 2:5-6
c) Jesus, quoting Micah 7:6 in Matthew 10:35-36

6. SIMILAR PASSAGES IN THE BIBLE
You may want to compare some passages of Micah which
are similar to parts of other books. Here are examples:

Micah	Other	Note
3:1-4	Amos 2:6-8	
6:1-5	Hosea 11:1-4	
chaps. 4-5	Zechariah 9-10	
3:9-12	Jeremiah 26:16-19	
4:1-5	Isaiah 2:2-5	
5:2-4	Matthew 2:1-6;	
	John 7:37-44	
7:5-6	Matthew 10:35-36;	
	Mark 13:12;	
	Luke 12:51-53	

Chart K

MICAH WHO IS LIKE JEHOVAH? 7:18

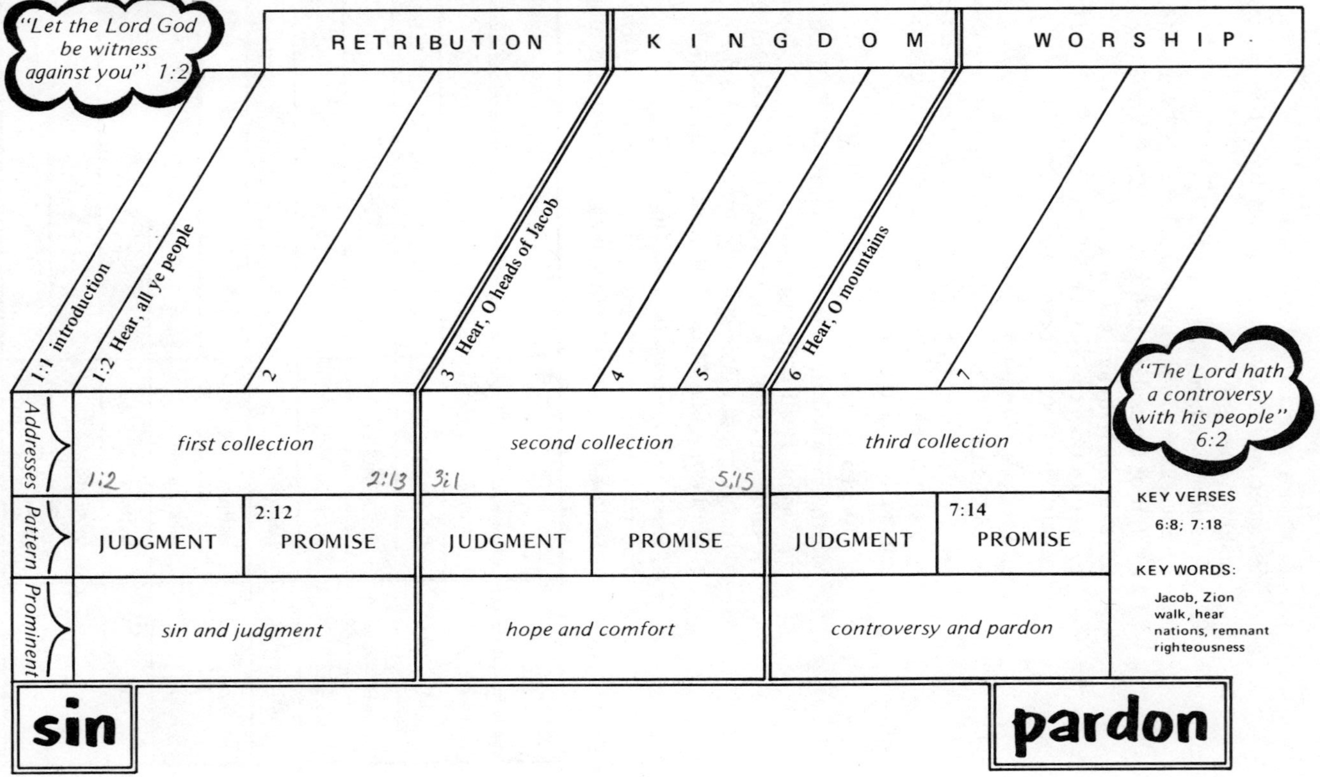

II. SURVEY OF MICAH

Follow procedures of survey suggested in the earlier studies of Obadiah and Joel. Then study the survey Chart K, which shows the structure of the book of Micah.

Note the following on the chart:

1. The book is of three main collections of messages.[1] Read the opening verse of each collection in your Bible. What parts of the verses are recorded on the chart?

2. What three-part outlines appear on the chart? According to these, how does Micah's theme progress throughout the book?

3. What pattern repeats itself in each of the three parts? Mark this in your Bible, scanning the text to justify such an outline.

4. Note other observations recorded on the chart, such as title, key words, and key verses.

5. Use the blank spaces at the bottom of the chart to add observations and outlines of your own at a later time.

* * *

Review Questions

p 43   1. What does the name Micah mean literally? How is that meaning reflected in the theme of the book?

p 44   2. What kings and prophets were living during Micah's time?

3. What happened to the Northern Kingdom during Micah's ministry? How would such an event affect his ministry to Judah?

p 46   4. How would you describe (e.g., good or evil) the reigns of each of the kings during Micah's time: Jotham, Ahaz, Hezekiah?

5. When did Micah probably write his book?

p 46   6. What is the main theme of the book?

p 47   7. Can you name six specific prophecies of Micah which have already been fulfilled?

p 48   8. How many collections of messages appear in Micah?

9. What subjects are prominent in each of these collections?

10. Quote a key verse of Micah.

1. Many Bible students see a main division beginning at 4:1 instead of 3:1. Also, some see this twofold structure: Denunciation, chaps. 1-3; Consolation, chaps. 4-7. This is similar to Isaiah's twofold makeup, and for this reason Micah has been referred to as "Isaiah in shorthand."

LESSON **6**

Micah 1:1—5:15

"Who Is Like unto Jehovah?"

THE FIRST WORDS OF MICAH SPEAK FOR

THEMSELVES: 'ATTENTION! LET ALL

THE PEOPLES OF THE WORLD LISTEN' (1:2).

And what the prophet wanted everyone to consider was the truth embodied in the *exclamation-question*: "WHO IS LIKE JEHOVAH!?"[1] Everything he said in the book was related in some way to this.

In this lesson we will be studying the first five chapters of Micah in detail. The lesson should be broken down into smaller study units, however, because of the length of the Bible text. Two natural units could be the ones shown earlier on the survey Chart K: 1:2—2:13 and 3:1—5:15.

I. PREPARATION FOR STUDY

1. Review survey Chart K, recalling the overall structure of Micah which you studied in the previous lesson. How often is the pattern of JUDGMENT-PROMISE repeated in the book?

2. Read Micah 1:1, which introduces the whole book. What does the verse teach about the following: source of the message; the messenger; time, extent and subject of the message?

II. ANALYSIS

Segments to be analyzed: 1:2—2:13; 3:1—5:15
Paragraph divisions: at verses 1:2, 8; 2:1, 6, 12; 3:1, 5, 9; 4:1, 6, 9; 5:2, 4, 10.

---

1. This double punctuation has been called an "interrabang." Try pronouncing the sentence to give the double impression which is intended.

50

A. First Collection: 1:2—2:13

1. Sin and Judgment: 1:2—2:11

Many phrases of this section are obscure in meaning. For this reason it would help you to use a modern paraphrase (e.g., Living Bible) along with the King James Version. (The study suggestions given throughout the lesson are based on the King James Version, unless otherwise designated.)

Read 1:2-7. What is the paragraph mainly about? _____

_____

What verse clearly tells the cause of divine judgment?

_____

Samaria was the capital of what kingdom? (See map.)

_____

When was the prophecy of Samaria's fall (1:6) fulfilled?

(Chart J). _____

Read 1:8-16. Micah ("I" of v. 8) here bewails the coming conquest of Jerusalem and its surrounding villages (vv. 9-16). The names of the villages are generally listed in a geographical order, from north of Jerusalem to the southwest. Micah foresees the Babylonian invader conquering town after town. In describing the invasion, he lets the literal meaning of each town's name suggest an aspect of the invasion. The verses might be paraphrased like this (beginning at 1:10b):[2]

Grovel in the dust at Dust Town (Aphrah).

There go the people of Fair Town (Saphir), in shameful nakedness.

The inhabitant of Outlet City (Zaanan) has no escape.

The foundations of Removal Town (Beth-ezel) are taken away.

The inhabitant of Bitter Town (Maroth) waits vainly for good.

Harness your steeds and away, O Horse Town (Lachish).

You must part with Possession Town (Moresheth).

And kings of Israel are deceived at Deceitful Town (Achzib).

2. See Ralph Earle, *Meet the Minor Prophets* (Kansas City: Beacon Hill, n.d.), p. 58.

The invader will inherit Hereditary City (Mareshah).
Israel's nobility will flee to the caves of Refuge Town
   (Adullam).

What is the last line of 1:16? When was Judah conquered by the Babylonians? (Chart D) _____

_____

Read 2:1-5. What kind of sin is exposed in verse 2? __

_____

Is this evil common today? _____

Read 2:6-11. According to verses 6 and 11, what kind of
a prophet did the people of Judah want? How does the

Lord rebuke them (vv. 7-10)? _____

2. PROMISE OF RESTORATION: 2:12-13

This short paragraph concludes Micah's first collection on
a bright note. Someone has likened it to "a ray of sunlight
streaming for a moment through the cloudy and dark day
of denunciation." Recall from your survey study that each
of the three collections ends on the note of promise (Chart
K).

This is probably a Messianic prophecy of the last days,
concerning believing Israel. (See Ro 9:26; 11:26.) The
"remnant" of 2:12 represents the believing Jews who will
survive the great Tribulation of the last days. (See *Notes*.) [3]

How is the "I" of 2:12 identified in 2:13? Note that
Micah describes a regathering (v. 12) before a triumphal
march (v. 13).

3. FOR THOUGHT AND DISCUSSION

1. Why do most unsaved people try to ignore warnings
about judgment to come? (See 2:6 and 2:11, TLB.)

2. What are the basic ingredients of the gospel message?
Is judgment included? If so, how?

3. Are social evils, such as oppression of the poor (2:2),
symptoms of something deeper in the sinner's heart?

4. In what sense is Israel being regathered today? Has
Israel had second thoughts yet about Jesus as their Messiah?

---

3. God has preserved a Jewish remnant of believers ever since the nation
   was formed in Abraham. (Cf. Ro 11:5.)

B. Second Collection: 3:1—5:15

This collection may represent several messages preached by Micah. On Chart L it is represented as two messages which follow the same *chronological* pattern: from the present time to the last days.

Read 3:1—5:15 paragraph by paragraph, referring to Chart L as you read. You may want to record your own paragraph titles in the oblique spaces, next to the ones shown. Study carefully the repeated chronological pattern on the chart.

Now concentrate your study on the first message, which runs from 3:1 to 4:8.

C. First Message: 3:1—4:8

1. SIN AND JUDGMENT: 3:1-12

Each of the three paragraphs (3:1-4; 3:5-8; 3:9-12) first describes the sins of the leaders (*now*) and then foretells judgment (*soon*). What is the judgment in each paragraph?

_____

_____

_____

Micah's prophecy of 3:12 was quoted over a hundred years later during Jeremiah's ministry (Jer 26:18). Read Jeremiah 26:10-19. Since Jeremiah specifically prophesied of the imminent fall of Jerusalem (586 B.C.), may it be said that Micah's prophecy of 3:12 was a reference to this judgment?[4]

Why do you think Micah inserted his personal testimony

at 3:8, in the middle of this message?[5] _____

_____

2. MESSIANIC KINGDOM: 4:1-8

Write a list of the various descriptions of the Messianic kingdom given by these verses.[6] Include what is said about

---

4. This event is called "soon" on the chart only in a relative sense. Actually the fall of Jerusalem was about 135 years distant.
5. The first words of 3:8 and 7:7 (ASV) are: "But as for me."
6. The Messianic kingdom is often referred to as the millennial kingdom. The word "millennial" represents the term "thousand years" which appears in Rev 20:2 ff. It will be a glorious kingdom with Christ as King, in fulfillment of the many promises given to Israel during Old Testament times. Most of the descriptions of this kingdom appear in Old Testament passages like this one.

PROPHECIES OF THE MESSIANIC KINGDOM
MICAH 3:1—5:15

Chart L

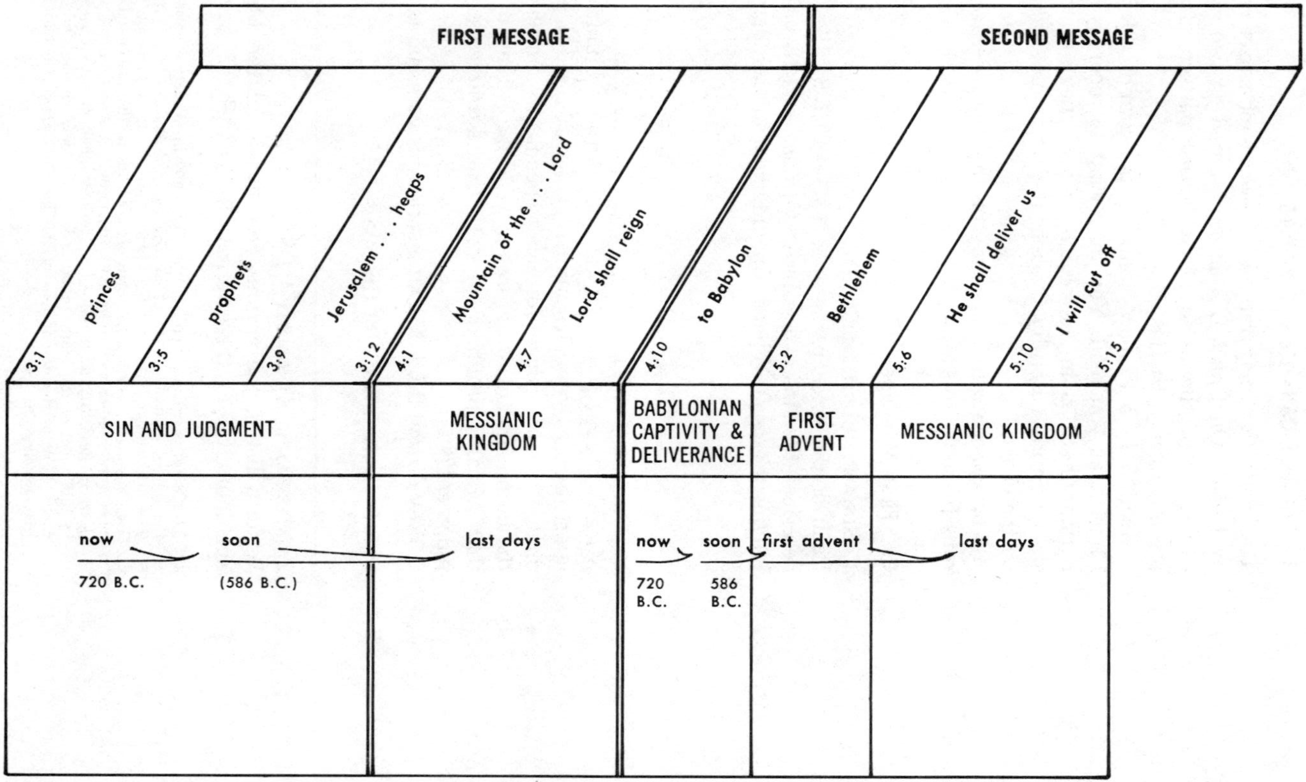

FIRST MESSAGE				SECOND MESSAGE		
3:1 princes	3:5 prophets	3:9 Jerusalem ... heaps	3:12	4:1 Mountain of the ... Lord	4:7 Lord shall reign	4:10 to Babylon	5:2 Bethlehem	5:6 He shall deliver us	5:10 I will cut off	5:15

SIN AND JUDGMENT	MESSIANIC KINGDOM	BABYLONIAN CAPTIVITY & DELIVERANCE	FIRST ADVENT	MESSIANIC KINGDOM
now 720 B.C. — soon (586 B.C.)	last days	now 720 B.C. — soon 586 B.C.	first advent	last days

the Lord; Jerusalem; the nation of Israel; Gentile nations.

Compare Micah 4:1-3 with Isaiah 2:1-4. Recall from Lesson 5 that Micah and Isaiah lived about the same time.

D. Second Message: 4:9—5:15

1. BABYLONIAN CAPTIVITY AND DELIVERANCE 4:9—5:1
Note that this message begins with the time of Micah ("now") just as the first message had begun.

The fall of Jerusalem (586 B.C.) is prophesied in 4:9-10a and 5:1, and captivity in Babylon is prophesied in 4:10b. The remainder of the passage is about deliverance that follows captivity. Read 4:12-13 again. Do the descriptions seem to apply to the temporary restoration of Israel during Nehemiah's time, or do you sense a reference to a more extensive and enduring deliverance? Many interpret the verses as applying to the last days, when Israel will be delivered after experiencing the Great Tribulation.[7]

2. FIRST ADVENT: 5:2-3
Read Matthew 2:5-6; John 7:42; Hosea 3:5; and Matthew 1:1-17. What is especially outstanding about the fulfillment

of such a prophecy as Micah 5:2? _____

In what sense did the birth of Jesus open the way for a return of apostate Israel to the family of God (5:3b)?

(Note: *The Living Bible* paraphrases the last line of 5:3 thus: "Then at last the exile remnants of Israel will rejoin their brethren in their own land.")

3. MESSIANIC KINGDOM: 5:4-15
First read the entire passage. In view of 5:2-3, who is the

---

7. See Merrill F. Unger, *Unger's Bible Handbook*, pp. 421-22.

"he" of 5:4?_____ Keep this in mind as you interpret *when* the prophecies of 5:4-15 would be fulfilled. For example, is the reference to Assyria, in verses 5 and 6, about the times *before* or *after* Christ's advent in Bethlehem? The latter interpretation suggested by E. Leslie Carlson, would be figurative; "Assyria was the foe most feared in Micah's day, and it is here used to typify Israel's enemies."[8] Will Israel have enemies in the last days?

Mark in your Bible these possible renderings of the text to accentuate the time references:

5:4—"now": "at that time" (NASB)

5:7—"and the remnant": "then the remnant" (NASB)

Also underline "in that day" (5:10) in your Bible.

Have the following prophecies been fulfilled yet?

5:4—"now shall he [Jesus] be great unto the ends of the earth"

5:8—"the remnant of Jacob [saved Israel] shall be . . . as a lion among the beasts"

5:9—"all thine enemies shall be cut off"

On the basis of your answer to the above question, would you say that 5:4-15 describes a glorious kingdom *yet to come*?

III. NOTES

1. "Is the spirit of the LORD straitened?" (2:7). The word "straitened" here means "impatient."

2. "Remnant" (2:12). This word appears six times in Micah; fifty-nine times in the Old Testament prophetic books. Various Hebrew words are translated by the one word "remnant" in the Old Testament. Basically the meaning common to all is "remainder," or "what is left." "At first the word denoted a part of a family or clan left from slaughter, and later came to be applied to the spiritual kernel of the nation who would survive God's judgment and become the germ of the new people of God."[9] Compare these New Testament references to "remnant": Romans 9:27; 11:5.

8. *The Wycliffe Bible Commentary*, p. 858.
9. *The Zondervan Pictorial Bible Dictionary*, p. 711.

3. "The breaker" (2:13). Berkeley Version translates this as "the breachmaker," that is, one who opens the breach to make a way through. Jesus as Messiah fits this picture perfectly, as taught in various New Testament passages (e.g., Heb 9:12).

4. "I will cut off thy horses" (5:10). That is, "I will destroy all the weapons you depend on" (TLB).

IV. FOR THOUGHT AND DISCUSSION

1. Leaders of Israel were "supposed to know right from wrong" (3:1, TLB). Are leaders in Christian work today accountable for the lives of other people? If so, in what ways?

2. What evil motives can ruin the ministry of Christian workers today? (Cf. 3:11.)

3. What is intended by these words in the Lord's Prayer: "Thy kingdom come" (Mt 6:10)? Compare Micah 4:8.

4. Why did God choose a small, insignificant city, Bethlehem, as the place of Jesus' birth? Was God trying to say something about true Messiahship, as well as about His own ways of performing?
5. Why will Jerusalem be a key city in last times? What is its status now?

V. FURTHER STUDY

Various subjects for further study are suggested by the passage of this lesson. An example is a comparison of the three types of Jesus' ministries: Prophet, Priest, and King.

VI. WORDS TO PONDER

His threats are for your good, to get you on the path again. (2:7b, TLB)

The Lord's Controversy
with Israel

THIS LAST SECTION OF MICAH IS

A KEY PASSAGE OF THE WRITINGS

OF ALL THE TWELVE MINOR PROPHETS.

It clearly summarizes all the vital issues about man's estrangement from God. Micah refers to the situation as the Lord's "controversy with his people" (6:2).[1] In these two chapters we study such basic subjects as the following:

Why man is separated from God

What God requires before there is restoration

The difference between religion and true worship

The principle of judgment for sin

Why God's pardon for sin is man's only hope.

1. PREPARATION FOR STUDY

1. Review survey Chart K to recall how this third collection of messages concludes the book of Micah.

2. Read 6:1-2, which introduces the Lord's "controversy" or lawsuit, with His people. Even nature is called upon to witness, if not judge, the confrontation. Chart M shows how the dialogue proceeds throughout the controversy.

3. Read the two chapters paragraph by paragraph, following the progression on Chart M as you read. Justify each part of the outlines shown next to the empty boxes. In how many paragraphs is the Lord the speaker? In the empty boxes record key words and phrases in each paragraph. This will help you see the *prominent* parts of the Bible text.

II. ANALYSIS

Segment to be analyzed: 6:1—7:20

1. See *Notes.*

THE LORD'S CONTROVERSY WITH HIS PEOPLE

(MICAH 6:1—7:20)

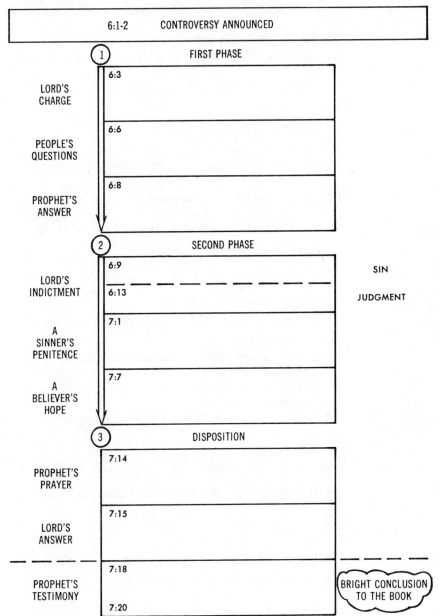

6:1-2	CONTROVERSY ANNOUNCED

① FIRST PHASE

LORD'S CHARGE — 6:3

PEOPLE'S QUESTIONS — 6:6

PROPHET'S ANSWER — 6:8

② SECOND PHASE

LORD'S INDICTMENT — 6:9 / 6:13 — SIN / JUDGMENT

A SINNER'S PENITENCE — 7:1

A BELIEVER'S HOPE — 7:7

③ DISPOSITION

PROPHET'S PRAYER — 7:14

LORD'S ANSWER — 7:15

PROPHET'S TESTIMONY — 7:18 / 7:20

BRIGHT CONCLUSION TO THE BOOK

Paragraph divisions: at verses 6:1, 3, 6, 8, 9; 7:1, 7, 14, 15, 18. (Mark these in your Bible. The study suggestions given below are starters to help you analyze the Bible text.)

A. Lord's Charge: 6:3-5
In your own words, what is the Lord's complaint here?

_____

_____

B. People's Questions: 6:6-7
How many questions appear in these verses? Were these honest questions on the part of the unbelieving Israelites?

_____

Did not the Israelites' Bible command the people to offer sacrifices to God (e.g., Lev 1:3)? What would cause God to reject the people's sacrifices? (Read Ps 51:16-19, which was another part of the Jews' Bible.) _____

_____

C. Prophet's Answer: 6:8
This verse has been called the "John 3:16 of the Old Testament." Why? _____
What does the verse teach about that which God
    reveals:
    requires:
    restores:
Compare the emphasis of *heart* in this verse with *ritual* in verses 6-7. _____
Also read Matthew 23:23; Ephesians 4:1-2.
    Do the commands "do," "love," and "walk" suggest salvation by works? If not, what do they teach you? _____

_____

D. Lord's Indictment: 6:9-16
What does the paragraph teach about sin (6:9-12) and judgment (6:13-16)? _____

_____

E. A Sinner's Penitence: 7:1-6

Do you see anything of repentance here? _____

F. A Believer's Hope: 7:7-13

This paragraph has many key phrases which adorn the matchless doctrine of salvation. (E.g., "I will look unto the LORD.") Make a list of these and, if you are studying with a group, discuss them. _____

_____   _____

_____

G. Prophet's Prayer: 7:14

What is the prayer of the prophet, in your own words?

_____

_____

H. Lord's Answer: 7:15-17

What is the Lord's answer? _____

_____

Apply this to the sinner, whose chiefest enemies include Satan, sin, and death itself.

I. Prophet's Testimony: 7:18-20

This passage has been called "one of the most exquisite things to be found in the entire Old Testament." What is the prominent subject of these verses? _____

_____

Why is such a testimony an appropriate conclusion to the book of Micah? (Recall the title which was assigned to the book, on the survey Chart K.) _____

_____

III. NOTES

1. "Controversy" (6:2). The root of the Hebrew word gives the picture of grappling and wrangling. Compare Genesis 26:20, where the same word is translated "strive." Also, compare Genesis 6:3, which uses a similar word for "strive."

2. "The land" (7:13). The New American Standard Bible translates "the earth."

IV. FOR THOUGHT AND DISCUSSION

1. What are unsaved people indebted to God for? Does God speak to people in ways other than by Scripture? (Ro 1:19-23.)

2. Why did God give the world a Bible? How does He speak to the world through His Son Jesus? (See Heb 1:1-4.)

3. Does God have a rightful claim on the lives of all people (6:8)?

4. What is genuine repentance? What part does it play in the conversion of a sinner?

5. Does the effectiveness of prayer depend on your believing that God hears your praying (7:7)?

6. In what ways has the Lord been a "light" to you personally since you became a Christian (7:8)? Have you had opportunities to share such a testimony with others?

7. What do these words mean to you: "Thou wilt cast all their sins into the depths of the sea" (7:19)? Do you think the intent is that God overlooks sin, or that no judgment or penalty is involved? Why did Christ die? Whose sins did He bear on the cross? Ponder the truths suggested by this familiar hymn:

> Alas, and did my Saviour bleed?
> And did my Sov'reign die?
> Would He devote that sacred head
> For such a worm as I?
> At the cross, at the cross where I first saw the light,
> And the burden of my heart rolled away,
> It was there by faith I received my sight,
> And now I am happy all the day!
>
> Isaac Watts

V. FURTHER STUDY

You may want to spend more time comparing Micah 6:8 with what the New Testament teaches about how a person is saved (e.g., Ro 3:21—5:21).

*   *   *

A CONCLUDING THOUGHT

Micah fully believed the *God could claim all, because He gave all*. This conviction gave him all the impetus he needed to preach the Word of the Lord, even though most of his hearers turned away. Are you standing up for Jesus, come what may? How would you apply this unfinished sentence to your own life:

"But as for me, I will . . . (7:7, NASB).

Nineveh Is Doomed

OVER A HUNDRED YEARS AFTER JONAH
PREACHED TO NINEVEH, GOD SENT ANOTHER
PROPHET, NAHUM, TO PRONOUNCE ITS DOOM.

The book of Nahum demonstrates how false is the view that "might makes right." The great Assyrian Empire, of which Nineveh was the capital, boasted its might and wealth, but it did not acknowledge its sin, nor would it listen to God. The fall of such a haughty nation was inevitable, as we shall see in our studies of this lesson.

I. PREPARATION FOR STUDY

1. Review Chart A, noting especially when Jonah and Nahum ministered as prophets. Jonah was a prophet of Israel whom God sent to preach to Nineveh. Nahum was a prophet of Judah, whose ministry also involved Nineveh.

2. Read Jonah 1:1-2 and 3:1-10. What was Jonah's message, the people's reaction, and God's response? Was a specific destruction of Nineveh foretold?

3. "So the people of Nineveh believed God" (Jon 3:5). In about how many years would this generation of believers have been replaced by the succeeding generation?

4. Read Nahum 1:1. What does this introductory verse suggest as to what Nahum's message is about? Now scan the remainder of the book to get the feel of the prophet's burden.

5. Note: Because of its length, this lesson should be studied in short sections. Three suggested units are: (1) background, (2) survey, (3) analysis.

II. BACKGROUND OF THE BOOK OF NAHUM

Now let us focus our attention on the original setting of Nahum's book. This will help to illumine our study of the text later in the lesson.

A. The Man Nahum

Very little is known of the personal life of Nahum. His name does not appear at any other place in the Bible (unless he is the Naum of Lk 3:25).

1. NAME
The name "Nahum," which is a shortened form of Nehemiah, means "consolation" or "comforter."

2. HOME
According to 1:1, Nahum was from a town called Elkosh. Four possible locations of Elkosh have been suggested: (1) in Assyria, north of Nineveh; (2) southwest of Jerusalem; (3) somewhere in Galilee; (4) the site of Capernaum (Caper-naum). Wherever Nahum's home was, we should keep in mind that when he was born[1] the Assyrian armies had already invaded Palestine twice:

> 722 B.C.—conquest of the Northern Kingdom (Israel) by Sargon II (2 Ki 17:6)
>
> 701 B.C.—invasions against Judah by Sennacherib (2 Ki 18:13-18)

3. TIME
Chart N shows the contemporary leaders of Nahum's day. Refer to it as you answer the questions below.

a) During Nahum's ministry three kings ruled over Judah. Who were they? Whose was the righteous reign? (See Chart D.)

b) Which was the ruling world empire of Nahum's time?

c) Which Assyrian king was reigning during the earliest years of Nahum's ministry?

d) When did Nineveh fall? What empire succeeded Assyria as the world power?

e) What other prophets were ministering around the time of Nahum?

---

1. The year of Nahum's birth is unknown, but he was probably younger than 50 when he began his prophetic ministry.

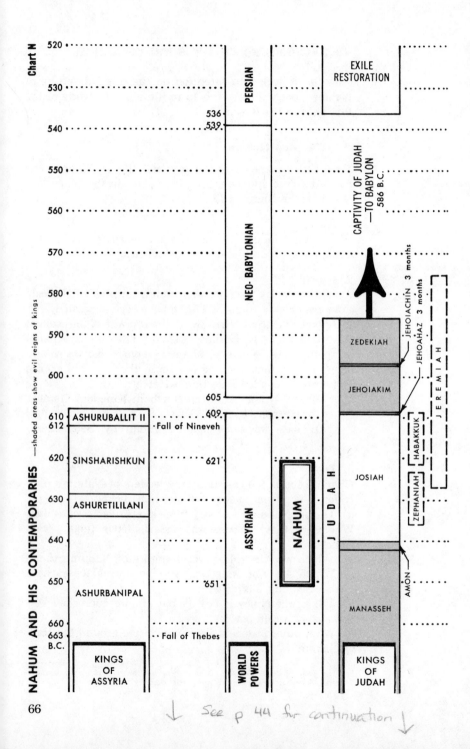

NAHUM AND HIS CONTEMPORARIES

—shaded areas show evil reigns of kings

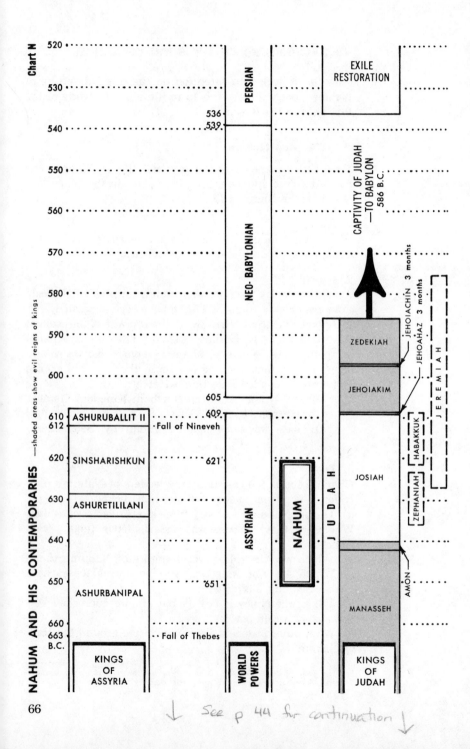

Chart N

KINGS OF ASSYRIA

B.C.	
610	ASHURUBALLIT II
612	
620	SINSHARISHKUN
630	ASHURETILILANI
640	
650	ASHURBANIPAL
660	
663	

WORLD POWERS

PERSIAN

536
539

NEO-BABYLONIAN

605

409 — Fall of Nineveh

ASSYRIAN

NAHUM

621

651

Fall of Thebes

KINGS OF JUDAH

EXILE
RESTORATION

CAPTIVITY OF JUDAH
—TO BABYLON
586 B.C.

ZEDEKIAH

JEHOIAKIM

JOSIAH

MANASSEH

JUDAH

JEHOIACHIN 3 months
JEHOAHAZ 3 months

JEREMIAH

HABAKKUK

ZEPHANIAH

AMON

66

↓ See p 44 for continuation ↓

4. KINGS AND CITIES

A few things should be noted concerning some rulers and cities directly related to the book of Nahum.

a) King Ashurbanipal. He was the last of the famous kings of Assyria. After his death (633 B.C.) the power of Assyria faded away. Ashurbanipal was exceptionally cruel. Skinning captives alive, forcing a prince to wear around his neck the bloody head of his king, and feasting with the head of a Chaldean monarch hanging above him, are examples of the gruesome stories about this tyrant.

b) King Josiah. Josiah reigned over Judah in the fear of the Lord. Read 2 Kings 22:1—23:28. Nahum may have written his book during Josiah's reign.

c) Nineveh. This was the capital of Assyria. It was founded around 2000 B.C. During Nahum's ministry it was at a peak of wealth, power, and fame. (Read 3:16-17.) The city walls were considered to be impregnable, yet Nahum prophesied their fall (e.g., 2:5-6). In 612 B.C. Nineveh was conquered and demolished by the Babylonians, Medes, and Scythians. The city has remained through all the centuries as a heap of desolate ruin.

d) Thebes. Thebes is the Greek name for the Egyptian city of No (Hebrew). (See 3:8.) The capital of Egypt, it was conquered by the Assyrians in 663 B.C. Nahum refers to this conquest in 3:10.

B. The Book of Nahum

1. DATE

Nahum wrote his book some time after 663 and before 612 B.C. This dating is based on his *reporting* of the fall of Thebes (3:10), which had already taken place (663 B.C.), and on his *foretelling* the fall of Nineveh (e.g., 2:8-10), which was still future (612 B.C.). Chart N shows Nahum's public ministry extending from about 650 to 620 B.C.

2. THEME AND PURPOSE

The theme of Nahum may be stated thus: The Lord, in His sovereign holiness and goodness, will bring judgment upon sinful Nineveh, and spare righteous Judah. The book is mostly about Nineveh, the subject which the opening sentence (1:1) introduces. It is also addressed mainly to

Chart 0

NAHUM WOE TO NINEVEH!

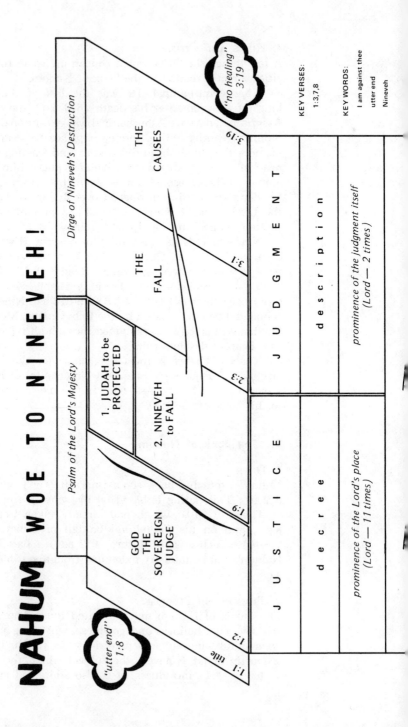

"utter end" 1:8

"no healing" 3:19

Psalm of the Lord's Majesty

Dirge of Nineveh's Destruction

GOD THE SOVEREIGN JUDGE

1. JUDAH to be PROTECTED

2. NINEVEH to FALL

THE FALL

THE CAUSES

title

1:1   1:2   6:1   2:3   3:1   3:19

J U S T I C E   J U D G M E N T

d e c r e e   d e s c r i p t i o n

prominence of the Lord's place (Lord — 11 times)

prominence of the judgment itself (Lord — 2 times)

KEY VERSES:
1:3,7,8

KEY WORDS:
I am against thee
utter end
Nineveh

68

Nineveh. It is the sequel to the book of Jonah. Do you think God would have withheld judgment of Nineveh if the people had repented of their sins, as their forefathers had responded to Jonah's message?

Nahum also wrote for the benefit of the people of Judah. He clearly answered questions raised by his brethren, such as:

Why does cruel Nineveh prosper?
Has God abandoned Judah?
Where is justice?

Do these questions have their counterparts in the world today?

III. SURVEY OF THE BOOK OF NAHUM

Chart O shows how the theme of Nahum progresses from its opening verse to the concluding one. Read through the entire book of Nahum, not slowly, referring to the chart as you read. You may want to record the outlines in your Bible before you do this scanning.
Note the following on Chart O:

1. There is a natural progression in the book. (See bottom of the chart. Also note the progression in the three sections, beginning with NINEVEH TO FALL.)

2. How is the first paragraph (1:1-8) set off from the rest of the book?

3. Study the four outlines which divide the book into two main sections.

4. How is Judah brought into the book? 2:2

5. Add to the list of key words as you proceed with your analysis of the text.

IV. ANALYSIS

Segments to be analyzed: 1:2-8; 1:9—2:2; 2:3-13; 3:1-19
Paragraph divisions: at verses 1:2, 9, 12b, 14, 15; 2:1, 3, 8; 3:1, 8, 15b.

A. God the Sovereign Judge: 1:2-8
Write a list of all the things said about the Lord in these verses. _____

_____

_____

Compare 1:2 and 1:7. _____

How does Paul apply the truth of Nahum 1:7 in 2 Timothy 2:19? _____

B. Nineveh to Fall and Judah to Be Protected: 1:9—2:2
In this passage Nahum alternates back and forth between the two subjects of judgment and deliverance. Record what each part says, in your own words:

1:9-12a   Nineveh: _____

1:12b-13[2] Judah: _____

1:14   Nineveh: _____

1:15   Judah: _____

2:1   Nineveh (See *Notes* on 2:1): _____

2:2   Judah (See *Notes* on 2:2): _____

C. The Fall: 2:3-13
In dramatic, picturesque language Nahum describes the imminent siege of Nineveh when her enemies come and utterly devastate the "impregnable" city. Read the descriptions verse by verse, and try to visualize each one. What

phrases strike you, for whatever reasons? _____

_____

D. The Causes: 3:1-19
More descriptions of the destruction of Nineveh appear here, but the main purpose of the passage is to show that Nineveh's *sins* are the *causes* of her judgment. Read the

2. The phrase "though I have afflicted thee" begins v. 12b.

verses and underline every reference to the evil ways of the Assyrians. (Some references may only be implied.) See if you can find references in addition to the following: verses 1, 4, 5-6, 16, 18, 19.

Try reading this chapter in *The Living Bible*, and you will catch something of the intensity of Nahum's prophecy about Nineveh.

V. NOTES

1. "A wicked counselor" (1:11). This may be one of the many references in Nahum to the king of Assyria. Note the specific reference in 3:18: "O king of Assyria."

2. "Though they be quiet" (1:12). The New American Standard Bible translates the middle of verse 12 thus: "Though they are at full strength and likewise many, even so, they will be cut off and pass away."

3. "Before thy face" (2:1). *The Living Bible* paraphrases the opening lines of 2:1 in this way: "Nineveh, you are finished! You are already surrounded by enemy armies!"

4. "The LORD hath turned away" (2:2). "The LORD will restore" (NASB).

5. "He shall recount his worthies" (2:5). "He [the king] remembers his nobles" (NASB).

6. "Huzzab" (2:7). This may be a reference to a queen (Berkeley), or the Hebrew may be intended as a verb, in which case a translation might be: "It is decreed." The American Standard Version reads: "And it is decreed: she is uncovered, she is carried away."[3]

7. "The bruit of thee" (3:19). That is, "the report of thee."

VI. FOR THOUGHT AND DISCUSSION

1. What place does righteous wrath have in the life of a Christian? What are your reactions to these comments:

> Surely there is a place for a book like Nahum even in the revelation of Grace. Instead of taking the Book of Nahum out of the Bible, we had better leave it there. We need it. It reminds us that love degenerates into a vague diffusion of kindly

3. Some see the word as a reference to Nineveh's patron, Ishtar, goddess of love and war.

feeling unless it is balanced by the capacity of a righteous indignation. A man who is deeply and truly religious is always a man of wrath. Because he loves God and his fellow men, he hates and despises inhumanity, cruelty and wickedness. Every good man sometimes prophesies like Nahum.[4]

2. When God decrees judgment for sin, He (always, never, sometimes) provides a way of escape. (Choose the word that best completes the statement. Justify your answer.)

3. How may the gospel be likened to news about the downfall of one's enemy? (Compare Nah 1:15 and Ro 10:15.)

VII.   FURTHER STUDY

Try writing your own modern paraphrase of Nahum 1:2-8, with a particular age group in mind (e.g., teenagers). What is the difference between a strict translation of the Bible and a free paraphrase?

*   *   *

A CONCLUDING THOUGHT

What are you thinking of, Nineveh, to defy the Lord? (Nah 1:9a, TLB).

4.   Raymond Calkins, *The Modern Message of the Minor Prophets* (Harper, 1947), p. 86.

ZEPHANIAH

God's severe judgements vs Judah 2-18

Day of the Lord's wrath
Day of the Lord's joy

day

Background and Survey
of Zephaniah

ZEPHANIAH WAS ONE OF JUDAH'S LAST

PROPHETS BEFORE THE NATION

FELL TO THE BABYLONIAN INVADERS.

Josiah, who reigned over Judah during Zephaniah's ministry, was the last of the righteous kings of this Southern Kingdom. How sobering it is to think of the people's accountability to God, for being ruled by such a righteous king and instructed by such faithful prophets as Zephaniah. In this lesson we will be studying more about this setting, and then we will survey Zephaniah's book as a whole.

I. BACKGROUND

Before going any further in your study, read the three chapters of Zephaniah in a scanning way. This will take the book out of the "stranger" category for the studies that follow.

Now look at the setting of Zephaniah's writing by following its antecedents in a chronological order. Chart P shows this historical background as well as Zephaniah's vision into the future.

Note on the chart the eight significant points, numbered consecutively. Refer to the chart as you study carefully each of the following eight descriptions:[1]

1. *King Hezekiah.* He was one of Judah's righteous kings. He may have been the Hizkiah of Zephaniah 1:1. If so, he was the great-great-grandfather of Zephaniah, the only prophet with royal blood.

2. *Birth of Zephaniah.* If the prophet was about Josiah's age, he was born around 648 B.C. (cf. 2 Ki 22:1). This was during the wicked reign of Manasseh. The name Zephaniah means "hidden, or protected, by Jehovah." Could it be that

---

1. Review Chart A to see Zephaniah's place among all the Old Testament prophets.

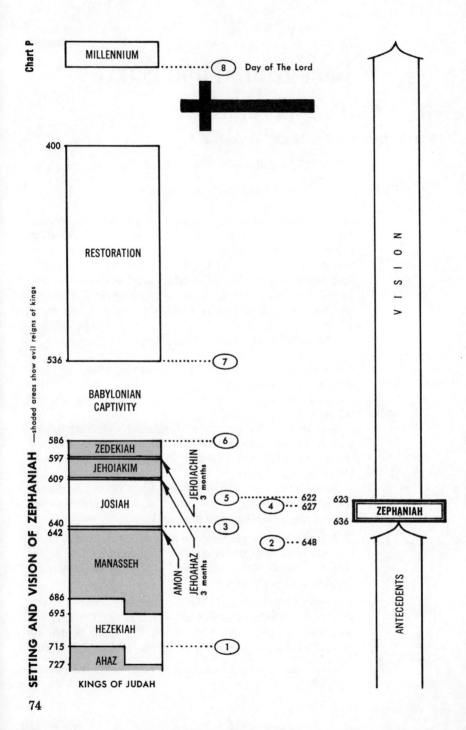

SETTING AND VISION OF ZEPHANIAH — shaded areas show evil reigns of kings

Chart P

MILLENNIUM .... (8) Day of The Lord

RESTORATION

400

536 .... (7)

BABYLONIAN CAPTIVITY

586 ZEDEKIAH .... (6)
597
JEHOIAKIM
609
JEHOIACHIN 3 months

JOSIAH .... (5) 622
(4) 627

640 .... (3)
642
AMON
(2) ... 648
JEHOAHAZ 3 months

MANASSEH

686
695

HEZEKIAH

715 .... (1)
AHAZ
727

KINGS OF JUDAH

ZEPHANIAH
623
636

VISION

ANTECEDENTS

74

his parents gave him this name in gratitude for his life being spared during the atrocities of King Manasseh (2 Ki 2:16; cf. Heb 11:37)? It is interesting to note that an important part of Zephaniah's message concerned the protection of Judah from harm in the day of God's judgment. (See 2:3.)

Zephaniah's home may have been in Jerusalem. Suggested dates for the term of his public ministry are 636 B.C. to 623 B.C.

3. *King Josiah.* Josiah was a great-grandson of Hezekiah (2 Ch 32:33; 33:20, 25). How then was Zephaniah possibly related to Josiah? Josiah was only eight years old when he began to reign over Judah (2 Ch 34:1). At age sixteen he "began to seek after the God of David his father" (2 Ch 34:3). It may very well be that Zephaniah's access to the royal court gave the prophet ample opportunities of witness to the king. In fact he may have been the key spiritual influence in Josiah's early life.

4. *The book of Zephaniah* (*c. 627* B.C.). It was during the early reign of Josiah that the prophet probably wrote his book, since there is no reference in the book to Josiah's reform program of 622 B.C. (For example, the idolatrous practices condemned in 1:3-6 were dealt with in the reforms.)

5. *Josiah's reforms.* At age twenty Josiah began a six-year program of national reform (2 Ch 34:3), which was completed in 622 B.C. (2 Ch 34:8). Read 2 Chronicles 34-35 or 2 Kings 22-23. The sins which Zephaniah condemns in his book were the sins over which Josiah lamented.

6. *Fall of Jerusalem* (*586* B.C.*)* Zephaniah also prophesied judgments for Jerusalem, the first destruction coming about a half century later. His prophecies also referred to judgments of succeeding centuries up to the last days. (This is an example of multiple prophecy, commonly found in the Old Testament.)

7. *Restoration* (*536* B.C *ff.).* Zephaniah also prophesied restoration of the chosen nation of God's people. This was fulfilled, at least in token measure, when God led His people back to the land at the end of the Babylonian captivity. But the full measure of restoration is yet to be. (This is another example of multiple prophecy.)

ZEPHANIAH DAY of DESOLATION and DELIVERANCE

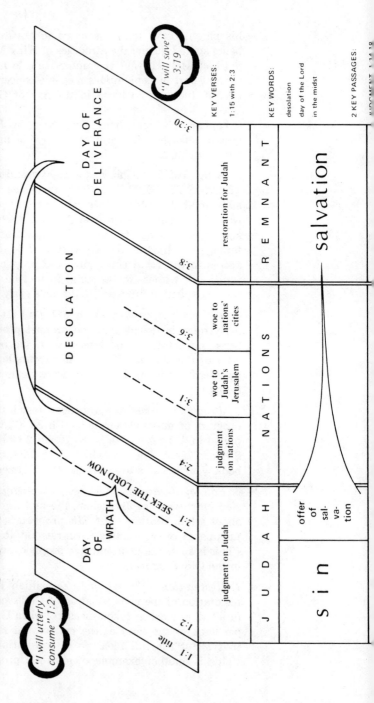

"I will utterly consume" 1:2

"I will save" 3:19

DAY OF WRATH		DESOLATION		DAY OF DELIVERANCE
1:1 title	judgment on Judah	judgment on nations	woe to Judah's Jerusalem	woe to nations' cities	restoration for Judah
J U D A H		N A T I O N S		R E M N A N T
s i n	offer of sal-va-tion			salvation

SEEK THE LORD NOW 2:1

1:2   2:4   3:1   3:6   3:8   3:20

KEY VERSES:
1:15 with 2:3

KEY WORDS:
desolation
day of the Lord
in the midst

2 KEY PASSAGES:
JUDGMENT 1:14-18

8. *Final "Day of the Lord."* The end-times judgments of the Day of the Lord will usher in the Messianic kingdom (millennium), when Zephaniah's prophecies of restoration will be fulfilled on a grand and total scale. Review Chart F and the discussion of Lesson 3 about the Day of the Lord. Recall that this day was a prominent subject of Joel's prophecy.

Be sure you are well acquainted with the eight points just discussed before moving on to the survey of the Bible text.

II. SURVEY

First, mark the following paragraph divisions in your Bible at verses 1:1, 2, 7, 14; 2:1, 4, 8, 12; 3:1, 8, 14.

Earlier in the lesson you scanned the three chapters of Zephaniah. Now, with pencil in hand, read the book once or twice more, underlining key words and phrases as you read. What repeated phrases strike you as very prominent in this book?

What is Zephaniah's message mainly about? Compare the opening verses (1:2-6) with the closing ones (3:14-20).

Chart Q is a survey of the structure of this book. Learn it well before moving on to the next lesson.

1. What is the function of the opening verse (1:1)?

2. How many main divisions in the book does the chart show? Mark your Bible to show the new divisions beginning at 2:4 and 3:8.

3. The title of the chart reflects the keynote of Zephaniah. Read the two key verses cited on the chart. What two outlines develop the subject of the Day of the Lord? What does this tell you about the day? (The word "day" in the phrase "day of the LORD" does not refer to a 24-hour solar day. Rather, it is an extended period of time, whether weeks, months, or even years.)

4. How much of the prophecy deals with Judah? How much deals with Gentile nations?

5. What makes possible a day of deliverance in Zephaniah's prophecy? Observe the function of 2:1-3, as shown on the chart.

6. Compare your answer of question 5 with the conditions which a sinner today must fulfill to appropriate the blessings of the gospel.

7. Read the Bible text to account for the two short sections beginning at 3:1 and 3:6.

8. Note the chart's contrasting phrases taken from the opening and closing of the book. Also, read in your Bible contrasting messages of the text: JUDGMENT: 1:14-18 and RESTORATION: 3:14-17.

9. Note the key words listed on the chart. Add to this list as you continue your study in the book.

* * *

Review Questions

1. What does the Hebrew name "Zephaniah" mean literally?

2. How was Zephaniah related to kings Hezekiah and Josiah, if at all?

3. Where was Zephaniah's home?

4. What kind of a king was Josiah?

5. About how old was Zephaniah when Josiah's reform program was completed in 622 B.C.?

6. Did Zephaniah write his book before or after Josiah's reforms?[2] Support your answer.

7. What are the two main prophecies of the book of Zephaniah? To what extent have they been fulfilled already? When will they be totally fulfilled?

8. What spiritual lessons can people today learn from Zephaniah? Do you think it is possible that God can raise up a modern "prophet" today to influence the course of a nation even as He used Zephaniah to influence Josiah and Judah?[3]

---

2. A project for further study is to inquire into how effective and enduring was Josiah's reform program.

3. Such a prophet would not be another "writing" prophet, of course.

78

Day of the Lord's Wrath

NO HUMAN BEING CAN FULLY COMPREHEND

THE AWFULNESS OF THE COMING

DAY OF THE LORD'S WRATH.

Today when newspapermen report catastrophes such as earthquakes and floods, they are at a loss for words to describe what they see. But the tragedy of such cataclysms does not compare with that which is yet to come, when God's judgment will fall in all kinds of ways upon unrepentant sinners. The passage of this lesson is Zephaniah's descriptions of that day, when God will "utterly consume all things from off the land" (1:2). Only a stony heart of unbelief is unmoved by Zephaniah's prophecy.

I. PREPARATION FOR STUDY

1. Review Chart Q, observing the places which the two segments 1:1—2:3 and 2:4—3:7 fill in the book of Zephaniah. Whom are the two segments about?

2. Read 1:1. Who was the source of Zephaniah's message?

3. Could anyone else originate such a prophecy? Recall from earlier lessons that the Day of the Lord is an extended period of time.

II. ANALYSIS

Segments to be analyzed: 1:2—2:3 and 2:4—3:7
Paragraph divisions: at verses 1:2, 7, 14; 2:1, 4, 8, 12; 3:1

A. Judgment on Judah: 1:2—2:3

Read 1:2-18 and observe the many references, direct or indirect, to the people and places of Judah. (Note: The phrase "the land" refers to Canaan, the land of the Jews.)

Recall that the passage is identified on Chart **Q** as JUDAH.

If you have not already done so, underline in your Bible every appearance of the word "day" and of the phrase "day of the LORD."

1. How thorough are the judgments of 1:2-3? _____

_____

2. The cause of judgment is always sin. What sins are referred to in 1:4-6? (See *Notes* on 1:5*b*.) _____

_____

3.
4. How often does the word "punish" appear in 1:7-13? What three groups of people are the objects of the punishment?

_____

_____

5. Make a list of the many descriptions of divine judgment in 1:14-18. _____

_____

_____

6. What one reference to judgment's *cause* is given in these verses? _____

_____

7. The "nation" of 2:1 is Judah. The phrase "O nation not desired" could read "O shameless nation." What does this tell you about Judah? _____

_____

8.
9. What phrases of 2:1-3 tell you that deliverance for Judah was possible? What are the three commands of these verses? _____

_____

_____

Observe on Chart **Q** how 2:1-3 is shown to relate to the last section of the book (3:8-20). What transforms one's destiny from a day of wrath to a day of deliverance? _____

B. Judgment on Nations: 2:4—3:7

1, First read 2:4-15 to observe references to geography. What verses record the names of these nations:

Philistia _____ Ethiopia _____

Moab _____ Assyria _____

Ammon _____

Observe on the map "Geography of the Minor Prophets of Judah," where these nations are located. Zephaniah's view moved from west (Philistia) to east (Moab and Ammon) to south (Ethiopia) to north (Assyria). Observe on the map also the four cities mentioned in 2:4. Where is

2 Nineveh (2:13) located? _____
What phrases of 2:4-15 suggest how intense the judgments

3 will be? _____
Note how often the word "desolation" is repeated.

4 What paragraphs record *causes* for God's judgments against the nations? Record the causes:

5 2:4-7 (Philistia) _____

6 2:8-11 (Moab and Ammon) _____

2:12-15 (Ethiopia and Assyria) _____

6 How is Judah brought into the description of Philistia's

judgment in 2:6-7? _____
Does this imply a cause for Philistia's judgment? (Cf.

7 2:9*b*.) _____

Read 3:1-5. Do the descriptions (e.g., of prophets,
priests) suggest that Jerusalem is the city of these verses?
8 Then read 3:6-7, and note that cities of the nations are
involved here. Observe how this is represented on Chart **Q**.

81

This, then, is the alternating pattern which Zephaniah follows in the four parts of 1:2—3:7:
a) judgment on Judah (1:2—2:3)
   b) judgment on the nations (2:4-15)
c) judgment on Judah's capital city (3:1-5)
   d) judgment on the nations' cities (3:6-7)

l̦ What is prominent in 3:1-5: *description* of judgment, or

cause of judgment? List the many causes cited. _____

_____

Note the reference to the Lord "in the midst" in 3:5. See also 3:15, 17.

2 What does the Lord say about judgment and its causes in

3:6-7? _____

_____

Think back over 2:4—3:7. Is any conditional offer of deliverance given to the nations? If not, why not? (Recall

3 the offer of deliverance to Judah in 2:1-3.) _____

_____

III. NOTES

1. "The remnant of Baal" (1:4). This refers to the remaining traces of Baal worship in Israel. The Canaanite nature-god Baal was represented by many Baals (Baalim). Read Judges 2:11-13; 6:28-32.

2. "Fish gate" (1:10). Verse 10 describes invaders coming upon Jerusalem from the north. The fish gate was at the northern edge of the city. The New American Standard Bible translates "the second" of verse 10 as "the Second Quarter" (i.e., of Jerusalem). Read this verse in the Living Bible.

3. "Men that are settled on their lees (1:12). H. A. Hanke comments, "Lees are dregs or sediment deposited from wine or liquor (cf. Is 25:6). To settle on one's lees meant to become complacent and self-satisfied with one's character and circumstances."[1]

1. H. A. Hanke, "Zephaniah," in *The Wycliffe Bible Commentary*, p. 885.

4. "Wrought his judgment" (2:3). A clearer translation is "carried out His ordinances" (NASB).

5. "Cherethites" (2:5). This was a tribe of people living in southern Philistia, whose ancestors may have come from the island of Crete.

6. "The coast shall be for the remnant of the house of Judah" (2:7). A multiple fulfillment of this prophecy may have included all these three occupations of Philistia by Jews:

a) in 586 B.C., when the Babylonians allowed some Jews to remain in the land
b) at the return of Jews from exile in Babylon (538 B.C. ff.)
c) in the end times

IV. FOR THOUGHT AND DISCUSSION

1. Why is it necessary, when studying a book of the Bible, to believe that the book was infallibly inspired? Do you believe Zephaniah's prophecies are wholly accurate?

2. What are some applications of 1:1—3:7 to today? What does this section of Zephaniah teach about God and man?

3. What is your definition of sin? Compare the phrase "against the LORD" (1:17) with 1 John 3:4.

4. Is sin a justifiable cause of the severe judgment described in Zephaniah (e.g., 1:17)?

5. If you are studying in a group, discuss the various kinds of sins exposed in 3:1-5. Are such sins common today?

6. Can a sinner become so hardened in his rebellion against God that any possibility of salvation is cancelled? Is there such a thing as "a point of no return" in his life, spiritually speaking?

7. How do you apply such prophecies as 1:2-6 and 2:1-3 to end times?

8. The Day of the Lord will be a day of judgment for some, and a day of deliverance for others. Relate this to Psalm 76:9.

9. Read 2 Peter 3:10-18. Note the appearance of the phrase "day of the Lord." What spiritual lessons can a Christian learn here in connection with the prophesied Day of the Lord?

10. What does it mean to you that the Lord is "in the midst" of His people (3:5, 15, 17)? Compare Revelation 1:13, 20. How does a believer sense the presence of the Lord? Why is His presence so vital?

V. FURTHER STUDY

1. Study what the New Testament teaches about the Day of the Lord.

2. You may want to inquire about what the Scythian invasion of Media and Persia in 632 B.C. had to do with Zephaniah's message, if anything. (See *The New Bible Commentary*, p. 737, and *The International Standard Bible Encyclopedia*, 4:2707.

VI. WORDS TO PONDER

I will . . . punish those who sit contented in their sins, indifferent to God, . . . thinking he will let them alone. (Zep 1:12, TLB).

Day of the Lord's Joy

ONE OF THE MYSTERIES OF THE

GOSPEL IS GOD'S GENUINE JOY IN

FELLOWSHIPING WITH REDEEMED SINNERS.

As dark as the book of Zephaniah is with its prophecies of divine judgment, the concluding verses resound with bright chords of joyful reunion. Let those skeptics who see the God of the Old Testament as a cruel tyrant and impersonal judge explain this verse:

> The Lord thy God in the midst of thee is mighty; he will save, he will rejoice over thee with joy; he will rest in his love, he will joy over thee with singing (Zep 3:17).

I. PREPARATION FOR STUDY

1. Review Chart **Q**, noting especially the place of 3:8-20 in the structure of Zephaniah's book.

2. Read these selected passages of Nehemiah which report the return of Jews to Palestine from the Babylonian captivity: Nehemiah 1:1—2:6; 2:17-18; 3:1; 6:15-16; 8:1—9:3; 12:27-30.

3. The tender love of God for His redeemed people is beautifully revealed by the Lord's own words recorded in Ezekiel 34:11-16, 19-21. Read these verses now.

4. Keep in mind this statement which was made in Lesson 3: Prophecies of the Day of the Lord are about a period of time at the end of the world when God's final judgments will fall upon unbelieving nations, and also when believing Israel will be delivered and blessed.

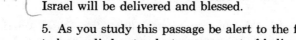
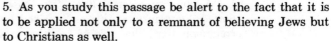

5. As you study this passage be alert to the fact that it is to be applied not only to a remnant of believing Jews but to Christians as well.

85

II. ANALYSIS

Segment to be analyzed: 3:8-20
Paragraph divisions: at verses 3:8, 14
Read the entire segment once, for first impressions, underlining prominent words and phrases as you read. Compare
verse 8 with verses 9-20, and record your observations
below:

	3:8	3:9-20
tone		
people involved		
what is prophesied		

Now read 3:9-13 again. May this have been prophetic of
Judah's return from Babylonian exile as well as a regathering to Palestine in the last days?

Read 3:14-20. What is there about these verses that
points only to the end times? For example, who but Jesus
must be the one meant by "King of Israel" in 3:15? What
does this Messianic passage teach you about the future dis-

position of a believing remnant of Israel? _____

_____

How many times does the phrase "in the midst of thee"
vs 15 17
appear in 3:8-20? What is meant by the phrase? _____

_____

What are the last three words of the book? _____

_____

III. NOTES

1. "A pure language" (3:9). The New American Standard Bible translates this as "purified lips." J. T. Carson
comments that "there would be those to whom God would

give a purified lip . . . so that they might all, Jew and Gentile (cf. Is. lxvi. 19, 20), call upon the name of the Lord in a new and better covenant, and serve Him with one consent."[1] Of this same passage Merrill Unger writes:

> The gift of a pure speech removes the curse of Babel (Gen 11:1-9) and anticipates the great outpouring of the Spirit (Joel 2:28-32), of which Pentecost (Acts 2:1-11) was an illustration.[2]

In this connection read Ezekiel 34:11-16.

2. "With one consent" (3:9). The Hebrew reads literally, "with one shoulder." The New American Standard Bible paraphrases, "shoulder to shoulder." The idea is that of togetherness in worship and service.

IV. FOR THOUGHT AND DISCUSSION

1. The first words of God to the elect people, the Jews, are recorded in Genesis 12:1-3. Read these verses. What prophecies of Zephaniah 3:8-20 perfectly fulfill the promises given in the Genesis passage?

2. Relate the passage of this lesson to Paul's prophecy of Romans 11:25-28 about what will happen to believing Israel in the end times.

3. Apply Zephaniah 3:8-20 beyond the immediate subject of Israel, for example, apply it to Christians. Here are suggestions:
a) What do the words "The LORD thy God" (3:17) mean to you as a Christian? How can Christian living reflect such a relationship?
b) What are your thoughts about how a Christian brings joy to the heart of the Lord? Try to locate verses in the Bible which speak of the Lord's joy (e.g., Ps 105:43; Jn 15:11).
c) What kinds of joy has Christ brought to you?
d) Reflect on the great truth of 3:15*b*: "Thou shalt not see evil any more." When will this be? Compare this prophecy with the descriptions of New Jerusalem in Revelation 21:1—22:5.

1. J. T. Carson, "Zephaniah," in *The New Bible Commentary*, p. 742.
2. Merrill F. Unger, *Unger's Bible Handbook*, p. 429.

4. The Old Testament prophets spoke more about the Messianic kingdom of the end times than about the earthly life of Jesus. Can you think of reasons why this was so?

* * *

A CONCLUDING THOUGHT

> An afflicted and poor people . . . shall trust in the name of the Lord (Zep 3:12).

> The common people heard him gladly (Mk 12:37).

Martin Luther has commented on Zephaniah's statement:

> He describes the Christian Church with few, but yet with most beautiful words; namely, that it is a poor, needy, and oppressed little people, that calls upon the Lord and trusts in Him, which is the highest righteousness and the most exalted worship. This is the true glory of the kingdom of Christ, that we are joyfully and in peace reconciled to God through Jesus Christ.[3]

3. Quoted by John Peter Lange, ed., *Commentary on The Holy Scriptures, Zephaniah*, p. 37.

HABAKKUK

complain of land's iniquity 1-4

~~which is shown~~

fearful vengeance of Chaldeans 5-11

complain tha vengeance is from those
    who are far worse 12-17

The Righteous man lives by faith

watchtower

Background and Survey of Habakkuk

HABAKKUK WAS THE LAST OF THE MINOR

PROPHETS OF JUDAH, AND WAS

TRULY 'A MAJOR MINOR PROPHET.'[1]

His book is only three chapters long, but it is filled with many spiritual gems for the Bible student. Your study of Habakkuk's message should prove to be a very stimulating and profitable experience.

I. BACKGROUND

We will approach the book of Habakkuk in the usual order of Bible study: first, background; second, survey; finally, analysis. This lesson involves background and survey. Before going any further in the lesson you may want to scan Habakkuk to catch something of its tone.

A. The Man Habakkuk
The little we know about the man Habakkuk is inferred from his short book. The name Habakkuk means literally *#1* "embracer."[2] Of this Luther writes:

> Habakkuk has a right name for his office. For Habakkuk means a heartener, or one who takes another to his heart and his arms, as one soothes a poor, weeping child, telling it to be quiet.[3]

The text of 1:1 identifies Habakkuk as a prophet, which *#2* in itself reveals much about his ministry. Some think his call to be a prophet came while he was serving as a Leviti-

---

1. So called by Frank E. Gaebelein, *Four Minor Prophets,* p. 142.
2. Read these verses where the same Hebrew word appears: 2 Ki 4:16; Job 24:8; Ec 3:5; Song 2:6.
3. Quoted in Gaebelein, p. 142.

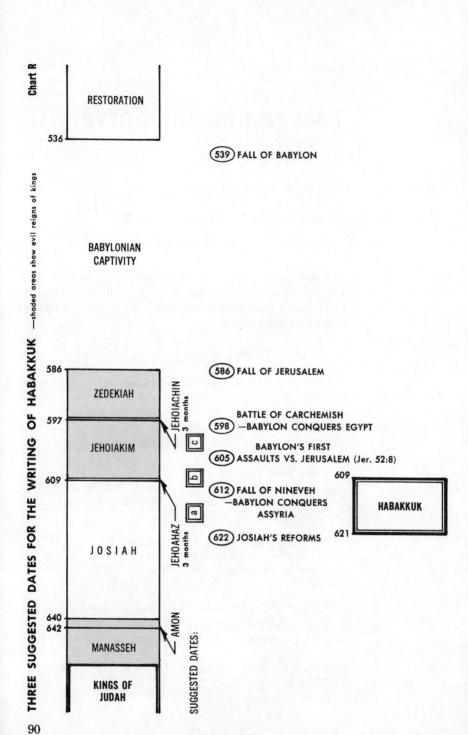

Chart R

THREE SUGGESTED DATES FOR THE WRITING OF HABAKKUK — shaded areas show evil reigns of kings

RESTORATION

536

(539) FALL OF BABYLON

BABYLONIAN CAPTIVITY

586

ZEDEKIAH

597

JEHOIAKIM

609

JOSIAH

JEHOIACHIN 3 months

JEHOAHAZ 3 months

(586) FALL OF JERUSALEM

BATTLE OF CARCHEMISH
(598) —BABYLON CONQUERS EGYPT

BABYLON'S FIRST
(605) ASSAULTS VS. JERUSALEM (Jer. 52:8)

c

b

a

(612) FALL OF NINEVEH
—BABYLON CONQUERS
ASSYRIA

(622) JOSIAH'S REFORMS

609

HABAKKUK

621

640
642

AMON

MANASSEH

KINGS OF
JUDAH

SUGGESTED DATES:

90

cal chorister in the temple.[4] This is suggested by the musical notations at 3:1 and at the end of the book: "For the choir director, on my stringed instruments" (3:19, NASB).[5] The prophecy of 1:6 points to the fact that Israel, the Northern Kingdom, had already gone into Assyrian captivity, for now the Chaldeans (Babylonians) were threatening Judah. Thus Habakkuk was a prophet of Judah.

After you have analyzed the book of Habakkuk, write a list of the prophet's character traits which you have observed in his writing.

B. Times in Which Habakkuk Ministered

Refer back to Chart N, which shows Habakkuk to be a contemporary of Jeremiah. There are various views as to exactly when Habakkuk ministered as a prophet and wrote his book, because the Bible text does not give direct information on this. The historical setting of Chart R suggests various possibilities of the book's date.

The three strong options for the date of Habakkuk are *a*, *b*, and *c* shown on Chart R: *a*—after Josiah's reform program (622 B.C.) but *before* Babylon (Chaldea) emerged as the threatening world power (612 B.C.); *b* or *c*—*after* Babylon emerged as the threatening world power (612 and 605). Of the two, *b* is the preferred view.

The spiritual condition of Judah when Habakkuk was ministering was one of dark apostasy (1:2-4). The fruits of Josiah's reform program must have been very temporary if a prophet of God would complain about national corruption only a decade later. Observe on Chart N that the last three kings of Judah were evil rulers. Read 2 Chronicles 36:14-16 for a description of the people's heart just before the Babylonians conquered Judah. Also read Jeremiah 10, which reveals Judah's sin of idolatry at this time. (Jeremiah, a contemporary of Habakkuk, was Judah's last prophet before the Babylonian captivity.)

C. The Book of Habakkuk

1. MESSAGE
Among the prominent teachings of the book are these:

4. Cf. 1 Ch 25:1. If this is so, his home was in Jerusalem.
5. Compare this reading with the paraphrase of *The Living Bible*.

a) Iniquity does *not* triumph.

b) God does not overlook sin.

c) The righteous man lives by his faith.

d) The Lord is God of the universe. Happy is the believer who waits patiently for the manifestations of His will.

e) God wants His children to talk with Him.

2. FEATURES

Some interesting features of Habakkuk include:

a) The book is similar to Jonah in that each book opens with the prophet plagued by a problem, and closes with the prophet having experienced God's solution.

b) A large proportion of Habakkuk (about two-thirds) is devoted to conversation between the writer and God.

c) A key verse of the book, 2:4, is quoted in three important New Testament passages. Read Romans 1:17; Galatians 3:11; Hebrews 10:38.

The truth of these verses was a keynote of the sixteenth-century church Reformation, and it is for this reason that Habakkuk has been called the "Grandfather of the Reformation."

d) The literary quality of Habakkuk is unsurpassed in the Hebrew Scriptures. Concerning chapter 3, Unger writes:

> The magnificent lyric ode of ch. 3 contains one of the greatest descriptions of the theophany in relation to the coming of the Lord which has been given by the Holy Spirit, awaiting fulfillment in the day of the Lord (cf. 2 Thess 1:7-10).[6]

II. SURVEY

A few suggestions for an overview of Habakkuk are given below.

1. Read through the book again, if you have not already done so. What words and phrases stand out as prominent ones?

2. Compare 1:1 with 3:1. Also compare 1:2 with 3:18-19. What are your observations?

3. Study the survey Chart S very carefully. The questions or suggestions given below are based on the chart.

---

6. *Unger's Bible Handbook*, p. 425. Definition: Theophany is an appearance or manifestation of God to man.

HABAKKUK THE RIGHTEOUS LIVE BY FAITH

QUESTIONS & ANSWERS	DECREES	PRAISE & TESTIMONY

1:1 intro | 1:2 | 1:5 | 1:12 | 1:17 | 2:1 intro | 2:2 | 3:1 intro | 3:2 | 3:3 | 3:12 | 3:16 | 3:19

HABAKKUK COMPLAINS

HABAKKUK LISTENS

HABAKKUK PRAYS

FIRST QUESTION

GOD'S ANSWER

SECOND QUESTION

GOD'S ANSWER

How long shall I cry? 1:2

I will rejoice 3:18

KEY VERSES
2:2,4,20
3:2

KEY WORDS:
Why
woe

93

4. Read each paragraph of the Bible text and record a paragraph title in each oblique space of the chart.

5. How much of the book records Habakkuk's words? God's words?

6. Note the three-part outline showing a progression of the prophet's mental attitudes.

7. Note the three-part outline at the top of the chart. Compare the introductory verses of each of those parts.

8. Why is the last chapter set apart so prominently from the first two?

9. Note the key words. Read the key verses in the Bible. Add to the two lists as you proceed with your study.

10. What are some spiritual applications already suggested through your study of this lesson?

*   *   *

Review Questions

p 89 1. What does the name Habakkuk mean?

p 89 2. How much is specifically known about Habakkuk's life and ministry?

p 91 3. Was Habakkuk a prophet to Israel or to Judah? Support your answer.

p 91 4. What approximate dates have been suggested for the writing of this book? What other prophet was a contemporary of Habakkuk?

p 92 5. What are some of the main teachings of Habakkuk?

6. How much of the survey chart can you remember without referring back to it in this study guide?

The Righteous Man Lives by Faith

TWO QUESTIONS WHICH PEOPLE KEEP

ASKING ARE: 'WHY DO THE RIGHTEOUS

SUFFER?' AND 'DOES JUSTICE TRIUMPH?'

God has given clear answers to the questions at various places in His Word, and the book of Habakkuk is one of these. Our study of this lesson will focus on this problem in the context of man's most desperate problem: death itself. "I want to live, but I must die" is the cry of man. "The righteous will live by his faith" is the redemptive response of God.

I. PREPARATION FOR STUDY

1. Although all of Habakkuk is the subject of this one lesson, it is recommended that you study the book in three study units. Let each chapter be a unit.

2. Refer to Chart S as you begin to analyze each chapter. For chapter 1, note on the chart that God's answer to Habakkuk's first question does not leave the prophet without another question.

3. Always keep a pencil or pen in hand while you are studying in order to mark your Bible and to record observations on paper or in this manual. This tool of Bible study really makes analysis come alive.

II. ANALYSIS

Segments to be analyzed: 1:1-17; 2:1-20; 3:1-19
Paragraph divisions: at verses 1:1, 2, 5, 12; 2:1, 2, 4, 6, 9, 12, 15, 18, 20; 3:1, 2, 3, 12, 16.

A. The Prophet Complains: 1:1-17

Read 1:1. What does the word "burden" suggest about the
ministry of a prophet? _____

1. _____

Read these verses where the same Hebrew word appears:
2 Kings 5:17; Psalm 38:4; Isaiah 46:1. Also compare
Galatians 6:2.

Read 1:2-4. What is the tone of the prophet's words?

2. _____

Is it fair to say that Habakkuk is complaining to God?
What is it that he is disturbed about? _____

3. _____

What does he mean by the words "the law is slacked"

4. (1:4)? _____

Read 1:5-11. This is the Lord's answer to Habakkuk's
complaint. Compare the tone of God's words (e.g., 1:5-6)

5. with that of the prophet's (1:2-4). _____

_____

What is God prophesying in 1:6? _____

6. _____

Why do people refuse to believe prophecy (1:5)? (Com-

7. pare Paul's quote of 1:5 in Acts 13:41.) doesn't want the
prophecy of old to come upon the beginning church
In what sense was the prophecy of a Chaldean invasion of
Judah intended to be a solution to Habakkuk's complaint
8. of 1:2-4? It tells what is yet to happen before things get
any better
Substitute the King James Version reading of 1:11 with
this translation:

> Then they will sweep through like the wind and pass on. But
> they will be held guilty, they whose strength is their god
> (NASB).

The key word of the verse is *but*. God says He will use
the Chaldeans to punish Judah, but—what? Keep this in
mind as you move now to Habakkuk's second question.

Read 1:12-17. This paragraph records Habakkuk's second question. (See Chart S.) How would you evaluate the prophet's faith at this point, according to 1:12-13*a* (up

to the word "iniquity")? *considers God his Lord* 9.

doesn't understand - seems unfair

The word "wherefore" of 1:13*b* means "why." Write this key word in the margin of your Bible. What problem was

still troubling Habakkuk, according to 1:13*b*? _____ 10

the wicked seem to be
in God's favor

B. The Prophet Listens: 2:1-20

God's answer to Habakkuk's second question is the subject of chapter 2.

Read 2:1. What mental and spiritual point has Habakkuk reached in his dialogue with the Lord? *wait for the*
Lord
faithful

Read 2:2-3. What references to time does the Lord

make in verse 3? *future* 2

Why is *time* a vital ingredient in the solution of the question about the triumph of justice? *time will eventually* 3
show the ans

Read 2:4-5. Compare the two different persons described here:

2:4*a*-5: *proud, haughty one* 4

2:4*b*: *righteous one*

(Note: Translate "just," v. 4, as "righteous." The same Hebrew word is translated "righteous" in 1:13.) Why do you think the Lord makes this comparison as part of His answer to Habakkuk? (Recall the prophet's words "the man that is more righteous than he" in the WHY question

of 1:13.) _____ 5

What foundational truths does 2:4*b* teach? _____
6

This is the key verse
Living by anything but faith is wrong
note: Prov 3:5,6

Why is the statement a key one in the Bible? (Cf. Ro 1:17; Gal 3:11; Heb 10:38.) our lives are based on this

Read the five *woe* paragraphs beginning at 2:6. How do these support what the Lord had said in 2:4-5? _____

Is God saying that evil nations like Babylon will eventually reap the consequences of their sin? For example, relate the prophecy of 2:8 to the fall of Babylon which came a half century later in 539 B.C. (Chart R). How is 2:20 a fitting climax of God's answer to the prophet? _____

Compare this verse with 2:14. _____

Who speaks the words of 2:20? If your answer is Habakkuk, is this his way to introduce his prayer and testimony of chapter 3? Also, how does the closing appeal ("let all the earth keep silence before him," 2:20) reflect Habakkuk's opening words: "I . . . will watch to see what he will say unto me" (2:1)? _____

C. The Prophet Prays: 3:1-19

"The quickest way to get on your feet is to get on your knees."

1. PETITION: 3:1-2

How did the Lord's answer of chapter 2 affect Habakkuk? _____

What is the prophet's prayer? _____

What do you think he means by "in the midst of the years"? _____

2. Ascription of Praise: 3:3-15
Read 3:3-11 (the Lord's dominion over nature) and
3:12-15 (the Lord's dominion over nations). What different things do you learn about the Lord from these two
paragraphs? _____

_____

3. Testimony: 3:16-19

Relate 3:16a to 2:1b. _____ /
What is so beautiful and heartwarming about Habakkuk's

testimony of 3:17-19? _____ 2
How does the testimony *hang* on the two words "although"

and "yet"? Compare Job 13:15. _____

_____ 3

Compare Habakkuk's heart attitude at the beginning of

the book with that of the end. _____ 4

_____

What do you think brought on such a change? _____ 5

_____

III. NOTES

1. "The law is slacked" (1:4). The New American Standard Version translates 1:4a thus: "The law is ignored and
justice is never upheld."

2. "For judgment. . . for correction" (1:12). The phrases
mean "to judge. . . to correct."

3. "My watch. . . the tower" (2:1). We do not know if
Habakkuk meant by this an actual tower. The purpose of
the mental and spiritual positioning was "to see what he
will say unto me." It is one thing for God to speak; it is
another thing for man to listen to Him. (Cf. Heb 1:1-2;
2:1.)

4. "Though it tarry, . . . it will not tarry" (2:3). Two
different Hebrew words are here translated by the one word

"tarry."[1] A paraphrase might be: "Though it may seem to linger because of your unanswered questions, it will not be behind schedule."

5. "The just shall live by his faith" (2:4). The following appears in the Amplified Bible as a footnote to this verse:

> There is a curious passage in the Talmud [the body of Jewish civil and religious law], which says that in the Law Moses gave six hundred injunctions to the Israelites. As these might prove too numerous to commit to memory, David brought them down to eleven in Psalm 15. Isaiah reduced these eleven to six in . . . 33:15. Micah (6:8) further reduced them to three; and Isaiah (56:1) once more brought them down, to two. These two Amos (5:4) reduced to one. But lest it might be supposed from this that God could be found in the fulfillment of the law only, Habakkuk (2:4) said, "The just shall live by his faith."[2]

6. "Shigionoth" (3:1). The singular form of this musical term, Shiggaion, appears in the heading of Psalm 7. The meaning is unknown.

7. "He will make my feet like hinds' feet" (3:19). *The Living Bible* paraphrases 3:19b thus: "He will give me the speed of a deer and bring me safely over the mountains."

IV. FOR THOUGHT AND DISCUSSION

1. Does God have a listening ear to complaint, of whatever sort it is? How did God react to Habakkuk's complaining?

2. Was Habakkuk a doubter?

3. What does the Bible teach about patience and endurance? See Romans 5:3-5. Why does God often move slowly in performing His work?

4. Compare Galatians 2:20 and Habakkuk 2:4.

5. What is the ultimate test of one's faith? Compare your own faith with Habakkuk's, as he testified in 3:17-19.

6. Compare Paul and Habakkuk as the two men are represented by their testimonies of Philippians 4:11-13 and Habakkuk 3:17-19.

1. See Strong's or Young's concordance.
2. The quotation is credited to William H. Saulez in *The Romance of the Hebrew Language* (1913).

COMPARISONS OF THE MINOR PROPHETS OF JUDAH

Chart T

Book	No. of chapters	A prominent symbol	A key phrase	A key verse	prophet's home town	prophet's name means	book's B.C. date
Obadiah	1	rock	"concerning Edom"	v. 15	a town of Judah	"servant of the Lord"	840–825
Joel	3	locusts	"day of the Lord"	2:21	Jerusalem?	"Jehovah is God"	820
Micah	7	plowshares	"What does the Lord require of you?"	7:18	Moreshath-Gath	"Who is like Jehovah?"	731–723
Nahum	3	bloody city	"burden of Nineveh"	1:8	Elkosh	"consolation"	650–620
Zephaniah	3	day	"day of the Lord's wrath"	1:15 with 2:3	Jerusalem?	"hidden by Jehovah"	627
Habakkuk	3	watchtower	"It will not tarry"	2:4	Jerusalem?	"embracer"	612–605

7. The word "salvation" is an important Bible word. How would you define salvation in the spiritual realm? Read Habakkuk 3:13, 18, where the word appears three times. The Hebrew is *yesha*, which is the origin of the name *Jesus*. Read Matthew 1:21. Why is Jesus the true Saviour?

8. For a final review of your study of the minor prophets of Judah, refer to Chart T, which summarizes various features of the books. Sometimes interesting observations are made when comparing similar things.

V. FURTHER STUDY

Spend more time comparing the three New Testament quotes of 2:4: Romans 1:17; Galatians 3:11; Hebrews 10:38.

*   *   *

A CONCLUDING THOUGHT

> And the Lord said to me, . . . Slowly, steadily, surely, the time approaches when the vision will be fulfilled (Hab 2:2-3, TLB).

Selected Sources for Further Study

Archer, Gleason L. *A Survey of Old Testament Introduction.* Chicago: Moody, 1964.

Baxter, J. Sidlow. *Explore the Book. Vol. 4.* Grand Rapids: Zondervan, 1960.

Davidson, F., ed. *The New Bible Commentary.* Grand Rapids: Eerdmans, 1953.

Douglas, J. D., ed. *The New Bible Dictionary.* Grand Rapids: Eerdmans, 1962.

Freeman, Hobart E. *An Introduction to the Old Testament Prophets.* Chicago: Moody, 1968.

Gaebelein, Frank E. *Four Minor Prophets.* Chicago: Moody, 1970.

Jensen, Irving L. *Independent Bible Study.* Chicago: Moody, 1963.

————. *Minor Prophets of Israel.* Bible Self-Study Guide. Chicago: Moody, 1975.

Lange, John Peter. *Commentary on the Holy Scriptures: Minor Prophets.* Grand Rapids: Zondervan, n.d.

Morgan, G. Campbell. *The Analyzed Bible.* Westwood, N. J.: Revell, 1964.

————. *Voices of Twelve Hebrew Prophets.* London: Pickering & Inglis, n.d.

Orr, James, ed. *The International Standard Bible Encyclopedia.* Grand Rapids: Eerdmans, 1952.

Payne, J. Barton. *Encyclopedia of Biblical Prophecy.* New York: Harper, 1973.

Pfeiffer, Charles F. *An Outline of Old Testament History.* Chicago: Moody, 1960.

————. "Hosea." In *The Wycliffe Bible Commentary,* ed. Charles F. Pfeiffer and Everett F. Harrison. Chicago: Moody, 1962.

Scroggie, W. Graham. *Know Your Bible.* Vol. I. London: Pickering & Inglis, n.d.

Strong, James. *The Exhaustive Concordance of the Bible.* New York: Abingdon, 1890.

Taylor, Kenneth N. *The Living Bible.* Wheaton: Tyndale, 1971.

Unger, Merrill F. *Unger's Bible Dictionary.* Chicago: Moody, 1957.

————. *Unger's Bible Handbook.* Chicago: Moody, 1966.

Whitcomb, John C. *Chart of Kings and Prophets.* Chicago: Moody.

Young, Edward J. *An Introduction to the Old Testament.* Grand Rapids: Eerdmans, 1949.

Young, Robert. *Analytical Concordance to the Bible.* Grand Rapids: Eerdmans, n.d.

Moody Press, a ministry of the Moody Bible Institute, is designed for education, evangelization and edification. If we may assist you in knowing more about Christ and the Christian life, please write us without obligation to: Moody Press, c/o MLM, Chicago, Illinois 60610.